# MUHAMMAD
## A BRIEF LIFE HISTORY

The Unlettered Prophet Who
Changed the World in 23 Years

## SYED IQBAL ZAHEER

Dar Ul Thaqafah

**Dar Ul Thaqafah**
www.darulthaqafah.com
https://twitter.com/darulthaqafah
Email: darulthaqafah@gmail.com

*Find our titles on your favourite online bookstore using the keyword 'Dar Ul Thaqafah'*

## Translation of the Qur'ān

It should be perfectly clear that the Qur'ān is only authentic in its original language, Arabic. Since perfect translation of the Qur'ān is impossible, we have used the translation of the meaning of the Qur'ān throughout the book, as the result is only a crude meaning of the Arabic text.

Qur'ānic verses appear in speech marks proceeded by a reference to the Surah and verse number. Sayings (Hadith) of Prophet Muhammad (saw) appear in inverted commas along with reference to the Hadith Book and its Reporter.

# CONTENTS

# INTRODUCTION

Numerous biographies of the Prophet of Islam exist in almost every language, but the life of the greatest benefactor of humanity is so fascinating that no excuse is ever needed for adding one's name to the honored list of his biographers. The author has presented a brief account of the great Prophet's life with special emphasis on his character and manners and has given a few of his sayings and miracles. A distinguishing  feature of the work is that it presents a brief yet integrated view of the Prophet's life which will, it is hoped, help in better appreciation of the message of the Prophet.

**S. Abul Hasan Ali Nadwi**
**Lucknow**

# FOREWORD

The life of the person whose biography is in your hands is not an easy one to narrate; especially if it has to be done in a few pages. For what he achieved with his forceful character in a short 23 year period has no parallel in history. Through what he brought, he not only gave a lasting turn to history, but also affected a revolutionary change in the life, manner, customs, and economic activities of a very large number of peoples on earth. Even up to this day he continues to influence, not unoften very phenomenally, lives of millions of people of all races and of all regions. In fact from this point of view his place among the family of great men stands totally unique. It is true that many other great men of the past continue to exercise influence over humankind to this day: men, such as Moses, Jesus, Buddha, and, to a lesser degree, some men of science and philosophy. But their influence is very nominal and limited compared to that of Muhammad on whom be peace. Further, their influences are continually waning. Whereas Muhammad's influence is gaining ground. His every single act of life, down to very small details, is imitated even in our times not by a few, but by millions of people all over the world from North America to the Moro islands. A full description of such a character, then, can not be an easy task. Further, he was a complete man  in the fullest sense of the word  who had his personality developed to such excellences as to render it inappreciable to those that are not themselves as well developed all round. Certain shades of his life, therefore, will always remain enigmatic to those that attempt to understand him. Nonetheless, no efforts to understand him will prove unrewarding.

Further, in attempting a brief account, we face an additional difficulty. He appeared in the full light of history and won to his side through his powerful character a people who hated him intensely at the beginning of his call. These people, to whom he later became dearer than their own souls, closely watched his every movement and noted down every word, down to such minor details as to what foot he chose to mount an animal, what names he liked most, what spot he selected to answer the call of nature during a certain journey and what were the lengths of his toes. These minor details, committed to writing with the precision of the exact words he employed when he spoke, and available to every modern critic, with all the particulars of the degree of authenticity of each report, in the form of thousands of *ahadith* (traditions), render it very difficult for one to choose a certain aspect of his life for elaboration without doing injustice to the rest and warping the whole. For instance, a single biography of the Prophet (that of Ibn Ishaq) written a hundred and fifty years after him would run into about 2500 pages of this size. And, even though it deals primarily with one aspect of his life, it is yet considered far from complete.

We shall, therefore, contend ourselves in this short work with the presentation  very briefly  of the history of what he brought: from the seeds to the fruits, from the first call to the final triumph, adding a short sketch of his character, followed by some of his sayings, prayer words, miracles, and, finally, predictions. We will have to, of necessity, ignore any description of what *it is* that he brought  however important it might be, leaving the serious student to seek the help of larger works.


**SYED IQBAL ZAHEER**

# Preface to the First Revision

When the book was first published in 1991, it wasn't foreseen at all that it would prove to be so successful on the stands. Within a month or so the first print had been bought out. Since then the book has been reprinted four times, with the demand still running high. The success can only be attributed to the popularity of the person itself whose biography it deals with. Muslims and non Muslims alike seem to be interested in him. Hence, when the question of a fifth reprint came, it was felt that addition of some more details would not be entirely uncalled for.

While the effort at the time of revision was to retain the original simplicity and brevity, such material was added as would throw light on a new aspect. The number of traditions quoted at the end has also been increased to forty (for the section to become an *"Arba`in"* by itself). A couple of illustrations, with some details that might be beyond the scope of this work, should prove to be of additional interest.

Hopefully, these have gone in the way of improving the work. *Wa Allahu waliyyu al tawfiq.*

**Syed Iqbal Zaheer**
**July 1995**

**Acknowledgment**
Although the illustrations in this book have been freshly prepared, acknowledgement is due to Dr. Hussain Mones, whose gigantic work *Atlas al 'Alam al Islami* (Al Zahra for Arab Mass Media Cairo), has been consulted with greatl profit.

# Chapter 1

# THE MAKKAN ERA

## THE BACKGROUND

The Arabian peninsula, excluding perhaps the Yemen, bears one of the harshest climatic conditions on the globe. Rainless the year around, temperature can be sizzling hot in summer and freezing cold in winter  both the seasons spanning almost half a year each. In the eastern and western flanks it can be very humid too. Add to that the dust storms that can last for days on, with the dust penetrating the best sealed rooms, and you have a full picture of a people under, so to say, an all round attack by the forces of nature. Only those that have a special reason to stay on, live in this land.

More than one quarter of the land is pure sand, insupportive of any form of life. The rest of the country is either naked mountains or land too arid for any kind of vegetation. There are no lakes or rivers and hence one can travel from one end of the country to the other but fail to find a single tall healthy tree standing on its own. It is only around some wells and springs that date palm oasis exist allowing some sort of sedentary life to a few: but such oasis too are few and far between.

Strange it is, yet, that at no time in history the land has been without people. Even Josephus, the most ancient historian, has mentioned the Arab lands, the Arab people and the ancient house of worship in Makkah.

All parts of the land have always remained populated, even if thinly, and even if by nomads who move with their camels following sparsely spread weeds and bushes. At the time of the Prophet, on whom be peace, Makkah happened to be the largest town. It was the religious, economic, and, the political center of the region, controlled by the Quraysh, by far the largest and most powerful of the tribes. These were idol worshippers and the guardians of the House of God  the Ka'ba  built about 4200 years ago by the great monotheist and prophet Ibrahim

(Abraham), on whom be peace. The House, however, now contained some 360 idols and attracted devotees from all parts of the land in yearly pilgrimage. The pilgrimage itself was a corrupt form of the one originally instituted by Ibrahim. Close by was the hill station Tayif. About 500 kilometers up in the north was Yethrib and at the same distance or little more down south lay Najran  two other note worthy large settlements in the western flank. The eastern flank had its own little independent Omani kingdom. The rest of the country was occupied by semi nomadic tribes  many a score of them  who zealously guarded their territory and exacted toll from passing trade caravans. Deep in the deserts lived the raw bedouins who depended on dates and camels and took to raid and plunder when continuous droughts deprived them of the two.

As stated earlier, the Makkans and those living in the surrounding areas were pagans. Yethrib had a large Jewish population, living there perhaps since before Christ  waiting for the last Prophet and the Messiah to appear, as prophesied in the Scriptures. They controlled commerce and agriculture mainly date and vegetable farms  of the area. The entire jewellery market was in their hands. After the Quraysh they were the next most powerful in trade, and, therefore, also culturally the next most influential.

The pagan Arabs who lived in Yethrib were largely farm laborers employed by the Jews. The Jews had also a settling in Khyber, a town some 200 km. north of Yethrib. The rest of the eastern flank was pagan  except for two tribes in the north of Hejaz that were Christian. Down in the south of Makkah, Najran was almost wholly Christian. It is said that they were in sufficient numbers to be able to raise an army of 100,000 troops at short notice.[1]

The eastern flank of the peninsula was also pagan. But the north  bordering the Roman Empire  was under considerable Christian influence. Yemen had a mixed population of Jews,

[1] One of the numerous valleys near Abha, not too far from Najran, was called *"Wadi Tathlith"*, (the Trinity Valley)  Dr. Hussain Mu nis, *Atlas `Alam al Islami.*

Christians and idol worshippers — each having successfully ruled the country at one time or the other. Across the sea was Habasha (Abyssinia), a Christian Kingdom. Egypt, Palestine and Syria were under Roman rule with perhaps half the population favorably inclined towards the religion of their masters. Iraq was divided between Romans and the Persians. The latter were fire worshippers and the second of the two super powers of the time.

The Quraysh of Makkah lived almost entirely by trade. During the pilgrimage season, fairs were held outside of Makkah where the tribesmen sold their wares to which the Quraysh added their own and in winters carried them to Syrian and Palestinian markets. In summer, they travelled down to the Yemen to buy spices and Indian goods downloaded on its harbors, and carried them to the northern regions, from where they were re exported to various parts of the Roman Empire. While returning, the Quraysh brought back food, clothes, arms and tools. Almost everyone of the Makkan region contributed his share of money, goods or efforts. At times the caravans could be as large as a thousand camels. Others of the eastern region either worked on small farms or became a link in the long chain of the age old spice, perfume and desert wares trade, between the Indian sub continent and Africa on the one side, and all parts of the Occident on the other, via Yemen, Hejaz, Palestine and Syria. Spices also reached Persia by the same ancient route.

Politically, the country was disunited to the last man. Not only in the deserts, to which the bedouins clung for freedom, even in the towns no government of any sort could hold the strongly individualistic Arabs together. They detested all authority, claimed equality to all men and respected only those tested in qualities of manliness, generosity, courage, magnanimity and uprightness, or, to use one comprehensive word in Arabic: *muru'ah*. Those who possessed these qualities became the *shuyukh* (singular: *sheikh*) who led the tribes by virtue of quality rather than authority.

The Quraysh of Makkah also commanded respect for the same reasons. In addition, they were of noble stock, noble breeding and noble carriage. Moreover, they were the guardians of the

House of God who fed and housed the pilgrims generously every year. But the authority of the Quraysh over the rest did not extend beyond settling minor disputes. All others were settled by the sword. Wars between the tribes were long and ferocious, for, the sense of honor and the energy to prop it were strong and inexhaustible.[2] Alliances were made and broken so fast that only a few understood who was fighting whom, on whose side and for what.[3] Even the Jews who lived a separate organized life in their walled settlings, freely fought each other, on the side of this or that Arab clan. Truly, it was a world where chaos and anarchy reigned supreme.

As an individual, the Arab was a man of strong and discernible traits. He wasn't the simple type that could be characterized and put into a slot. Yet, he wasn't hocus pocus also, or, shadowy and secretive. Rather, he was someone whom you might have cause to approve or disapprove, but you knew for sure, and whose behavior you could fairly accurately predict. He was perhaps so different because he wasn't attached to the earth, people, and norms. Almost always he was on his own, free and unrestrained, hence not the stereotype, artificial mass produced kind that those cultures need that produce humans as tools for building up the nation. Ready to wear kind of things therefore wouldn't fit him as each individual had to be measured individually and judged separately. Also, he could somehow exist on different levels, sliding down from one to the other with the felicity of a bird in the air diving down to another plane of the atmosphere   a trait that has led some people to think of them as of split personalities.

The quality that stood out most in him was his pride. What was he proud of anyway? Well, he was proud of being what he was! He was, for instance, proud of being an Arab, who could

[2] The *Bu'ath* war that had ended recently had lasted a hundred years.

[3] The Prophet seems to have had a good knowledge of the complex alliances, and the exact terms of the alliances between the dozens of tribes that inhabited the land during his times. This is apparent from the way he, later in Madinah, cut through alliances and isolated his unbending adversaries, destroying them singly.

survive the harsh Arabian climate. Further, he could speak Arabic: the language in which he could express himself so precisely and accurately; the language of nuances; the language of sense rather than the meaning; the language that gave the desert aristocrats of a keen perception, the words that no language can boast of; the language in which his poets produced those masterpieces that, (and, undeniably, the claim was not without some justification), no nation had produced.[4]

He was self confident, honest, straightforward and quick of intelligence. Yet, he was a man of decision who stood firm until his destruction.[5]

He was courageous and detested weakness. He was truthful as well as true to his word. Honoring the guest was his religion. But he drank heavily, and, when he was not trading, fighting, or saying erotic poetry, he was gambling. When he was somber, he was rational. He worshipped idols alright. But if it was a lean period, and the idols were made of dates, he ate them up without remorse. And although he had a deep sense of honor, which would not tolerate even a minor insult, or his wife as much as exposing her ankle to another man, it would not come in his way of losing his wife and children in gambling. It was his sense of honor taken to perverse ends that he buried his female child alive from fear of poverty or the shame of giving her away when she grew to another man's pleasure. Sex was

---

[4] *Zafa* in Arabic is for a bird which is flying in the sky making circles; *sabal* for the rain drops that have not yet hit the ground and *atfara* for making a horse jump from one bank of a stream to another: words useless to look for in other langugages. To give another example, for 'man' alone there are thirty descriptive words for various stages in life, from the embryo in the womb until death in old age.

[5] When a non Qurayshi, Abdullah ibn Mas'ud, placed his foot on the chin of the fallen Abu Jahal, a leader of the Quraysh, Abu Jahal expressed his deep anguish that he was being beheaded by a man of low status. And when a Muslim went into the trench during the battle of the Trench, to behead another fallen Makkan, he was told to apply his sword a little further down on the neck so that his head might stand out when placed among others!

easy and copiously indulged in,[6] and those who lived by the
"age old trade" did it openly and with full dignity. In contrast,
their, properly married women were generally chaste. And,
although he was a born aristocrat, he could be beastly too. He
drank wine in the skull of his enemy, whom he could fight
over a dispute involving the lineage of a horse. Intemperance
was his another characteristic, so that what he did he took
to extremes.

The religion too that he believed in gave him full freedom.
It didn't impose laws, taboos and fetishes, and did not interfere
with his private or public life. He (and even she) circumambulated
the Holy mosque nude, in fulfillment of oaths.

Nevertheless, it shouldn't be imagined that there was absolutely
no good in the individual or the society. There were individuals
and families that rose far above the common lot, and could
be measured by the standards set by any other culture and
society. Although, of course, they were as few as the oasis
and their moral impact on the masses was the same as that
of the oasis on the economy.

Surely, if the political, economic and the social conditions were
as ideally harsh for the new Prophet as one wishing to put
his abilities to test could imagine, the raw material of human
beings given to him was another and harsher test of his abilities.

## EARLY LIFE

Born posthumously in a Quraysh family to parents Abdullah
and Aminah in Makkah in 570 C.E. (Christian Era) Muhammad
led a simple life. Nothing unusual is reported of his early years
except that at the age of three when he was playing with another
boy, two angels descended upon him. They slit open his chest,
took out his heart, removed and threw away certain matter,
washed it and filling it with some other material replaced it
and resealed the chest. A lad who witnessed the scene reported

---

[6] In the words of Patai, "(An area of the world which) has always been
of high and intensive sexuality." Hammudah Abdullah `Ati, *The Family
Structure in Islam*, p. 47.

it to the nurse who could not elicit any other information and finding no evidence on the body of Muhammad attributed it to the work of the jinn.

He spent his boyhood as a shepherd and took to trade in manhood. He carried people's goods to Syria and other Middle Eastern places and shared profits with them. His fair dealings earned him the appellate: Al Amin (the trustworthy). Reports of his honesty also reached a wealthy widow Khadijah who entrusted her business to him. Impressed by his sincerity and integrity, this previously twice married, but even now much sought after lady, offered to marry him. Muhammad consulted his uncle and with his consent married her and moved into her house, for he had no house of his own. He was then 25 and she 40. They led a very happy life together. She gave him two sons who died in infancy and four daughters who grew to adulthood. We have no evidence that he married her for money. But the money did come handy. He liberated slaves, supported the poor, and helped the widows. Much later, Khadijah incidentally expressed satisfaction over the way he spent her wealth.

## FIRST REVELATION

Historical research shows that at no time of his life did Muhammad worship idols nor did he take part in the religious practices, rituals or celebrations of his time. Yet he was neither an iconoclast nor an outspoken critic of the deities. However, with advancing age, Muhammad gradually took to retreats in caves where he lived alone for short periods meditating upon his life and times, and to seek, as Haykal has put it, a new level of seriousness, wisdom and ethical goodness.

It was during such a retreat in a cave called Hira, three miles off Makkah, at the ripe age of 40[7] that angel Jibril (Gabriel) appeared before him and said: "Read." Muhammad was unlettered, so he said, "I cannot read!" The angel again

---

[7] It is in this age, when passions of youth start to cool down and the soul begins to search for new dimensions of life, that the soul drifts into new untried fields, or, retreats back to the physical world, to apply itself to it more rigorously, if no light is shone.

commanded him to read, and Muhammad repeated his answer. After the third time, the angel hugged him forcefully, almost squeezing him, and then pronounced the first revelation of God. It said:

*Read: In the name of the Lord who created.*
*Created Man of a blood clot.*
*Read: And thy Lord is the Most Gracious,*
*Who taught by the pen,*
*Taught Man what he knew not.*
(Chapter 96, Verse 1 5)

The angel departed, leaving Muhammad in fear, doubt and anxiety. He was unable to clearly make out what it meant. He descended and went home hurriedly. There, he related the incident to Khadijah expressing his apprehensions. By now Khadijah had lived with him for 15 years. She knew him very well. She said: "No! Be not afraid. God will not waste you away. For you help the widow, support the orphan and assist the wayfarer."[8]

Subsequently, she took him to an old man Waraqah who had given up idol worship, adopted Christianity and had gained considerable knowledge of the Scriptures. After hearing Muhammad he assured him that the angel was the same that had brought revelations to Moses. He bid Muhammad to stay firm and warned him that one day he would be exiled by his people.

After some time the angel appeared again and as Muhammad lay enwrapped in a mantle, revealed the following message:

*"O thou shrouded in the mantle,*
*arise and warn!*
*Thy Lord magnify, thy robes purify*
*and all abomination shun!*
*Give not, thinking to gain greater*
*and be patient unto thy Lord."*
(Chapter 74, Verses 1 7)

---

[8] Note that ihus Khadijah stated a rule.

8

# THE GENERAL CALL

The revelations ceased thereafter. Perhaps because Muhammad needed to get used to the electrifying experience. When they resumed after quite a long spell, they began coming down in regular intervals. The theme of these early revelations was: "Give up idol worship, serve one God alone, be just, honest and chaste. Give alms to the poor, the orphan, the slave and the wayfarer. Give up vile practices such as burying alive of the female offspring, oppression of women, slaves and the weak, slandering chaste women, killing innocent people and eating of the carrion. And be warned that all people shall be resurrected on an appointed day when scales will be set up, each man's deeds weighed and the virtuous rewarded with Paradise and the wicked punished with everlasting Fire." For example:

> "I swear by this city,
> this city in which you yourself are a dweller,
> by sire and offspring:
> indeed, We have created man in affliction.
> Does he think that none has power over him?
> "I have wasted vast riches", he says.
> Does he think that none observe him?
> Have We not given him two eyes,
> a tongue, and two lips,
> and shown him the two paths?
> Yet he has not attempted the Ascent.
> Would that you know what the Ascent is?
> It is the freeing of a slave,
> or the feeding, in a day of hunger,
> of an orphaned near of kin,
> or a needy man in misery.
> Moreover, it is to be of those who believe and counsel
> One another to be steadfast, and enjoin mercy on one another.
> Those who do this shall be on the right hand.
> And those who deny Our revelations
> shall be on the left hand,
> With Hell fire close above them."
> (Chapter 90, tr. M.A. Salahi & A.A. Shamis)

And,

*"When the Earth is rocked with her (final) quake,*
*When it shakes off her burdens,*
*and man cries: "what is the matter with her?"*
*On that day she will tell her news,*
*that your Lord would have inspired her (with His command),*
*On that day men will issue forth in small groups*
*to be shown their labors.*
*Whoever has done an atom's weight of good will see it then,*
*and whoever has done an atom's weight of evil will see it then also."*
(Chapter 99, tr. M.A. Salahi & M.M. Shamsi)

## THE RESPONSE

The first who accepted Muhammad's call were: Khadijah, Abu Bakr, his childhood friend, Ali, his cousin, and Zayd, his slave. Gradually, the drops became a trickle and would have been followed by mass conversions but for the Quraysh who rose up in alarm and took to active opposition. The chief cause of their opposition was Islam's rejection of the idols that were the object of worship since ages. The Quraysh, who had always taken pride in the greatness of their ancestors, could not suddenly turn around to denouncing the deities that their revered ones had worshipped. Surely it meant severing the link with their noble forefathers and putting themselves on par with the common folk. And, apart from the prospects of losing leadership of the people with the abandonment of the deities, the Quraysh also stood to lose the economic benefits that came by it. They thought that Muhammad (himself a Quraysh) could not see the point in his madness. Finally, the religion of the Prophet gave no importance whatsoever to the origin of the people, their race, language or social status. It valued only true piety. The lowest of the lowly who possessed the virtues preached by Islam were the most honorable in the eyes of the Prophet and the community of believers.[9]

---

[9] Several examples can be cited from the early Makkan verses of the Qur'an that deal with this subject. We relate here, however, for reasons

There were other reasons too why they opposed Islam. One reason was jealousy. When a man called Abu Jahal, the staunch opponent of Islam, was asked about his personal opinion of the new religion the Prophet was presenting, he said: "Look! We and the house of Banu `Abd Manaf have been competing for years. They housed the pilgrims, we too housed the pilgrims. They fed them, we too fed them. Now they say they have a Prophet. Now where are we going to produce a prophet from? By God we will never accept him." Yet another reason was pride. When the Prophet tried to persuade the same Abu Jahal while they were strolling through a valley, he responded by saying: "Muhammad. There isn't a man who walked past these hills nobler than me."

Therefore, after the first few years of indifference and ridicule, the Quraysh became critics and then opponents to the call of Muhammad. Their religion, culture, social system, political power, and economic advantages that they drew from the old system, seemed to be threatened. In other words the survival of Quraysh as Quraysh seemed to be under threat. Hence they stretched their arms of repression with full might.

## PERSECUTIONS

They tried to dissuade the Prophet from preaching his religion by offering him the choicest of maid in marriage, a large amount of wealth and, most important of all, permanent leadership of the Quraysh: in other words, kingship of Arabia. When he

of better illustrative value, a hadith of the Madinan period. Abu Hurayrah says the Prophet was asked as to who among the people was most honorable. "The most God fearing among you is the most honorable in the eyes of God", was the reply. "Not (about the qualities) of the people do we ask you", they said. "Then the most honorable was Yousuf (Joseph) who was the son of a Prophet, grandson of a Prophet, and great grandson of a Prophet", responded the Prophet. "Not of him do we enquire too", they said. "Do you then", he said, "ask me about the Arab clans?" "Yes indeed", they said. "The better among you then", he said, "are those that were good in the days of ignorance (pre Islamic days) if they now understand (Islam) well". (Bukhari and Muslim)

refused and warned them instead of the Hell fire that awaited
them if they remained intransigent they began to put pressure
on his clan to abandon him in order that they could do away
with him without fear of retaliation. But when they failed in
that they took to persecuting him and his followers. The weak,
the slaves and those unsupported by a tribe became easy targets.
On hot Arabian afternoons they laid them on burning sands
and had rocks placed on their chests promising them relief
only if they would repudiate the new religion. Some were rolled
in mattresses and choked with smoke. Others were chained
and dragged around in the streets. The Prophet himself was
spared such harsh treatment, because of the strength of his
clan, but he was prevented from preaching by the jeers, clappings,
and other forms of ridicule that accompanied him wherever
he went.

## THE BOYCOTT

The Quraysh, however, failed to win back a single convert or
halt the conversions completely. They decided, therefore, to
implement a complete social boycott and isolate Muhammad
and his clan, the Banu Hashim. The Makkan tribes signed
a treaty by which the Banu Hashim were to be blockaded in
a valley. They were not allowed to come out or take part in
trade or social ceremonies. They were not married to, nor could
give away their daughters in marriage. They could not even
purchase food. The Prophet and his clan was soon reduced to
chewing leather and eating grass, and would have met with
death through starvation had not some people from outside
secretly begun to smuggle in small amounts of food. The boycott
lasted three years but failed to break Muhammad or his followers.
It was at last lifted through the clemency of a few sympathizers
among the Quraysh. Persecution however continued in various
forms with the result that to accept Islam meant reckless
defiance of a ruthless populace.

## MIGRATION

With the opposition of the Quraysh unrelenting, the Prophet
allowed his followers to migrate to other countries. Around 200
migrated to Abyssinia (today's Ethiopia). The Prophet's son in

law and daughter  Uthman and Ruqaiyyah  also went with the first batch. The Quraysh sent a delegation to Najashi, the ruler of that country, to try and get them back but failed in their bid. In the meanwhile, two tribes of Yethrib, Aws and Khazraj, evinced interest in Islam and agreed to accept Muslim emigrants. The Prophet agreed to the emigration of Muslims to their dwellings and they began to move there in small numbers. These developments, and the fact that they could not enforce a complete halt to conversions, increased the anger of the Quraysh who first put a ban on his preaching within Makkah, and that not proving very effective, decided to do away with the Prophet himself and began to look for an opportune moment.

The Prophet was aware of their plans and began to look for a tribe that would protect him and allow him to preach among the masses. It was also necessary at this juncture because he lost  in the 11th year after the revelations began to come both his wife Khadijah and uncle Abu Talib. Khadijah was a source of moral support to him, while Abu Talib had, as the leader of his clan, all along shielded him from the Quraysh. The new leader of the clan was Abu Lahab, an uncle of the Prophet, but who was dead opposed to Islam. The Prophet, therefore, went to Tayif, a table land and summer resort about 80 Km. from Makkah, and appealed to its leaders. But they refused to talk to him. One of them said: "I'll tear the shroud of Ka'ba, if (it is true that) God has chosen you for Apostleship." Another man said: "Didn't God find anyone else for Apostleship save you?" And a third man said: "Look! I do not want to talk to you. For, if you are a true Prophet, then I'll land into serious trouble if I reject you, and if you are phoney, then, of course, it does not befit me to talk to you."

The Prophet requested them to keep their opinions to themselves, and let him preach among the masses. But they refused. Instead, they incited the urchins of the town to chase him out. They began to stone him and abuse him. When he sat down exhausted, they pulled him up again and forced him to walk, until he found sanctuary in a farm owned by two brothers 'Utbah b. Rabi'ah, and Shaybah b. Rabi'ah. He took some rest there and wiped his wounds. The intensity of pain he felt at being stoned out of town is well reflected in the prayer he addressed to God there:

*God! I complain to Thee of my weaknesses, want of means, and lowliness before the people.*

*God! Thou, the Most Merciful, Thou are the Lord of the weak, and Thou art my Lord.*

*God! Whom do You turn me over to? (consign me to???) To one afar who will misuse me? abuse me??? Or to an enemy whom You have given power over me?*

*But if You are not angry with Me, it does not matter to me.*

He returned from Tayif hurt and disappointed.

His entry into Makkah now depended on a clan taking him into protection. Without that his life was under threat. He presented himself to a number of people. But, against the tradition and against Arab sense of chivalry, they refused. For a moment it looked as if he would not be able to enter Makkah at all. Finally a man known as al Mut'im b. 'Adiyy agreed to take him into his protection. He girt his sword, and accompanied with his sons similarly armed, went to the Ka'bah and announced his protection. But the ban against the Prophet preaching within the city remained in force. Nevertheless, it did not apply to preaching outside of Makkah. A Makkan, however, accompanied him wherever he went to distract attention and prevent anyone from listening to him.

## PLEDGES AT 'AQABAH

One place where he could preach freely was Mina. It was at a distance of about five kilometers from Makkah. Here the pilgrims gathered each year to spend a couple of nights after the rites of hajj. Most of those whom the Prophet addressed refused to listen: under the pressure and threats of the Quraysh of course. When he used to call out: "People! Say there is no god save One God, and you will succeed," a Makkan would shout out: "People! Don't listen to this man. He will cast a spell on you." He approached several tribes here: Banu 'Amir, Ghassan,

14

Banu Fuzara, Banu Murra, Banu Hanifa, Banu Salim, Banu
`Abbas, Banu Nasr, Tha`laba b. `Ukaba, Kinda, Kalb, Banu Harith
b. Ka`b, Banu `Udhra, Qays b. al Khatim, Abul Hasir, Anas b.
Rafi` etc., to name some, to give an idea of the strenuous nature
of the Prophet's task.

When he presented his message to a tribe called Banu 'Amir
b. Sa'sa'ah, one of the men called Bayharah b. Firas remarked:
"By God, if I can win this young Qurayshi, I can overcome the
rest of the Arabs." Then he asked Muhammad, "Supposing we
were to give you our pledge and protect you, and you emerge
successful, will the leadership be conferred upon us?" The
Prophet told him, "This is for God to decide. He confers leadership
upon whom He wills." Bayharah said: "Are we to offer our necks
to the swords of the Arabs and non Arabs, and when you come
out successful, leadership goes to others? We are in no need
of such a deal."[10]

Another meeting with another tribe Banu Shayban makes
interesting reading. We reproduce the whole both for interest
as well as to show that it was not for the Arab tribes a simple
question of switching over from the worship of idols to the worship
of one God  although that too was a difficult decision to make.
But there were many other factors involved that had to be carefully
considered, especially that of how those in power, both inside
and outside Arabia, were going to look at a seemingly local
Arab affair. For the slightest acquaintance with the message
of Muhammad gave indications that this was something that
was completely opposed to all prevalent systems, whether
pertaining to the religious aspect of life or the social, economic
or political, and thus a challenge to all established systems.
And, it may be pointed out, the same holds good today.

However, in this case, Abu Bakr, who used to be with Muhammad,
first greeted the group of men that appeared very dignified and
well behaved. Abu Bakr spotted the youngest and the most
handsome of them, Mafruq b. 'Amr, and the following conversation
took place:

---

[10] *Sirah Rasulullah,* Ibn Ishaq, Tr. Alfred Guillaume.

Abu Bakr, "In what numbers are you?"

"A thousand. And a thousand will not be defeated because of fewness," Mafruq replied.

"And how is your provision," Abu Bakr asked.

"Well," he said, "We have good luck and bad luck."

"And how did the wars between you and your enemies go?" asked Abu Bakr.

"Well!" Said Mafruq, "We are the angriest when we meet our enemy, and the most difficult to be encountered, when angry. We give preference to our horses over our children, and arms to women (prisoners). As for victory, it comes from God. He grants it sometimes to us, sometimes to others."

Then he asked Abu Bakr, "Probably you are a brother of Quraysh?"

"Hasn't the word reached you," replied Abu Bakr, "about a Prophet that has appeared? (Then, pointing to the Prophet) Well, this is he."

Mafruq said, "The news has reached us." (Then turning to the Prophet), "What's your message, O brother of Quraysh?"

The Prophet came forward and said, "I invite you to the belief in one God who has no partners, and that I am His Messenger. I also seek your protection and help, for the Quraysh have suppressed the word of Allah and have cried lies to His Messenger propping up falsehood against Truth. Although, Allah is Self sufficient, Praiseworthy."

"What else is your message, O brother of Quraysh," enquired Mafruq. The Prophet read out the following verse of the Qur'an: "*Come, let me pronounce to you what your Lord has forbidden you: 'That you should not assign partners unto God, be kind to your parents, and do not kill your children from fear of poverty. We (ie. God) feed you. And them too. And don't approach obscenity: whether open or secret. And do not kill the soul which God has made sacred except by way of justice.' This is how God commands you, haply that you may use your reason.*" (The Qur'an, 6: 151)

"And what else is your message, O brother of Quraysh?" Mafruq enquired again.

In reply the Prophet recited the following verse of the Qur'an: "God commands justice, to do good, to give the (blood) relations (their due), and forbids you the obscene, the evil, and rebellion. He admonishes you that haply you may learn." (The Qur'an, 16: 90)

Then Mafruq said, "By God, you invite us, O brother of Quraysh, to the best of deeds. And the people who have rejected you and cried lies to you have done a great wrong." Then, it seemed he wanted Hani b. Qubaysa to take part in the conversation. So he said, "This is Hani b. Qubaysa, our chief and in charge of our religious affairs."

Hani said, "I have heard your conversation, O brother of Quraysh. And I can see that ourselves giving up our religion in favor of your's is something that will have neither a beginning nor an end. ... Troubles always accompany haste. Further," he added, "behind us are a people whom we do not want to commit to something (without their consultation). Therefore, you return and we return. You consider (further) and we shall consider (further)."

And, as if wishing to involve Muthanna b. Haritha  in the conversation, he said, "This is Muthanna b. Haritha, a chief and the commander of our forces."

Muthanna said, "I have heard your conversation, O brother of Quraysh. And my reply is the reply of Hani b. Qubaysa to the effect that our giving up of our religion in favor of yours is a matter that is going to have neither a beginning nor an end. Indeed that places us in a fix between the waters of Yamama and Samawah."

"(What do you mean by) the two waters?" the Prophet enquired. "I mean," said Muthanna, "the waters of the Persian (Emperor) Chosroes and the waters of the Arabs. What concerns with the waters of the Persian (Emperor) Chosroes, has its violator unforgiven and his excuses unacceptable. As to what concerns the waters of the Arabs, well, the sin is pardonable and the violator's excuse acceptable. As for us, well, we are under the pledge that we have given to the Persian (Emperor) Chosroes which we cannot violate nor can we shelter one who will attempt that. Also, let me tell you something. I personally see what you are presenting as something that kings and rulers would disapprove of. (So we will not risk ourselves fighting Chosroes). But, so far as the waters of the Arabs are concerned, we are prepared to offer you help."

(What he meant was that sheltering the Prophet would mean threatening the interests of both the Arabs and non Arabs, and he was prepared to face the Arabs but not the non Arabs). The Prophet told him, "Your rejection is not that hurtful when it is accompanied by such eloquence. However, God's religion will not be defended but by him who will agree to do it at all fronts."[11]

The Prophet was not so unlucky with the pilgrims coming from Yethrib. The first year six men came into the fold of Islam but kept the matter secret. The second year another 12 gave the pledge. These were of the Aws and Khazraj, two large tribes of Yethrib. They had often heard from the Jews living there that a Prophet was soon to appear with whose help they (the Jews) would annihilate their enemies. These men of Aws and Khazraj, therefore, once convinced, hastened to embrace Islam before the Jews would.

The second year's pledge at 'Aqabah in Mina is known as 'The Pledge of Women' for it involved no fighting for the defence of Islam. One of the participants 'Ubadah b. Samit relates: "We gave allegiance to the Apostle that we would associate nothing with God, not steal, not commit fornication, not kill our offspring, not slander our neighbor, not disobey him in what was right. If we fulfilled this, Paradise would be ours; and if we commit any of these sins, we should be punished in this world and this would serve as expiation. If the sin was concealed until the Day of Resurrection then it would be for God to decide whether to punish or to purify."[12]

11 *Fiqh al Sirah al Nabawiyyah*, Munir Ghadban, p. 276
12 *Sirah Rasulullah*, Ibn Ishaq, Tr. Alfred Guillaume

The next year another 70 men and two courageous women secretly converged at a hide out in small bands at 'Aqabah in Mina at the small hours of the night. This time they gave their pledge to defend the Prophet if he decided to emigrate to Yethrib. When one of those present, Al 'Abbas b. 'Ubadah b. Nadlah, warned them that by offering the Prophet a sanctuary among themselves, they were inviting the reds and the blacks to wars against them, their leader, Al Bara' said: "By Him who sent you with the truth we will protect you as we protect our women. We give our allegiance and we are men of war possessing arms which have been passed on from father to son."[13]

They asked him what they would get in return. The Prophet promised them Paradise. They said, "Stretch forth your hand." When he did that, they pledged their word.

Although kept secret, the news of their conversion could not be hidden from the Quraysh for long. They were already uneasy about the Muslims' migration to Yethrib.

Now they began to get the inkling that Muhammad might follow them. A series of consultations took place between their leaders and finally it was decided that in the darkness of night a group of people representing all the clans should bring down their swords jointly on Muhammad so that the responsibility of the murder would not fall upon any single clan leading to blood feuds.

## HIJRAH

The Prophet received the news about the plot to murder him probably through revelation and the same night he left for Yethrib with Abu Bakr and a guide. The Quraysh found Ali sleeping in his place and sent scouts all across the country with 40 camels as the price for his head. But the Prophet went down south instead of north and hid in a cave for 3 days. Then as the search for him cooled down a bit, he emerged and taking a new route and traveling waywardly reached Yethrib safe and sound. After that the town came to be known as Madinatu An Nabiyy (the city of the Prophet) or simply Madinah.

[13] Ibid

# Chapter 2

# THE MADINAN ERA

## THE MADINAN CLIMATE

The hijrah (migration) was a major turn in the history of Islam. The Islamic calendar dates from this year (A.H.= After Hijrah) which took place 13 years after the revelations began, that is, when the Prophet was 53 years of age. His age itself was no mean figure. Surely, much more than the average age of the time. Therefore, for all intent and purposes he was past the prime of life, and in that part of the age when a man likes to withdraw to an easy chair and brood over the past. Whoever wants to make a fresh start at this age? And, with the umbrella of defense provided to him by the Madinans, the chapter of pain, sufferings and tribulations seemed to have ended, and he should have quietly accepted a life of retirement. Muslims too felt free to move about, do business and follow their faith without fear of persecution or insult. However, things were not to be so, neither for the Prophet nor for them, as we shall see presently.

Now, as pointed out earlier, before the Prophet's emigration, Madinah was a conglomeration of small localities or dwellings. It consisted mainly of five large tribes: two Arab, Aws and Khazraj, and three Jewish, Banu Qaynuqa', Banu Nadir and Banu Qurayda. These divided themselves again into families or clans and lived in small or large groups with sufficient empty or cultivated lands between them. Major Jewish clans lived in walled dwellings. Aws and Khazraj had been at war with each other since over a century and were quite exhausted of fighting. The Jewish tribes also took sides and quite often slit each other's throats fighting for this or that party. They were, however, a dominant force. They had a great part of the cultivable lands in their possession wherein worked the peasants of Aws and Khazraj. They had the Madinan commerce in their control, both by way of agriculture and trade as well as their traditional profession: banking. They accepted not only property and weapons, but also women and children as security, whose ownership was transferred with the default of payments. Finally, they were esteemed high for being the People of the Book. They had come to Arabia from Palestine fleeing Christian persecution and following the prediction that the last Prophet was to appear in the Hejaz.

When the Prophet announced his office they were taken by surprise and were beset with doubts. They had not thought he would be an Arab. They had expected that he would be Jewish, even if appearing in Arabia. In reaction they first tried to predict, applying the "science of numbers" to the Qur'anic verses as to how long the Prophet's message would last. The figure came to a happy 71 years. But, learning of similar occurrence in the Qur'an, they reached a figure of 734, which was a bit more than they would allow, so they abandoned the exercise.[14]

Their basic problem was of course that they wanted dominance over the people. They had made a pact with God to this effect: they must have a special place, and they must give the world its religion  Abrahamic, based on "Divine" Law, to themselves and Noachide, based on "natural" moral laws to others.[15]

Hence they demanded, even as they do today, a special and honored place among the family of mankind. What the Prophet was presenting fell far short of the Jewish requirements. Far from giving them the right to choose other's religion, it was commonly known that the Prophet did not accept even social superiority of a people over others on the basis of color, race or nation. In Islam all were treated equal and brothers unto

[14] The Arabs have assigned numbers to each of their alphabet letters. *Alif* for instance is equivalent of 1, *lam* is equal to 30, *kaf* has been assigned the number 10, *qaf* has 100 etc. Working by the numerical value of certain verses, some Jews predicted that the Prophet's reign would last 71 years, and hence unworthy of a following. But other verses gave them much hig er figures which confused them. See Ibn Hisham.

[15] See the essay *Islam and Christianity in the Perspective of Judaism* by Michael Wyschogrod in *Trialogue of the Abrahamic Faiths* ed. Ismail R. Faruqi. (American Trust Publications).

each other. Only those who were God fearing won honor and respect. Moreover, after initially facing Jerusalem in Prayers, the Prophet received orders through revelation to orient himself towards Ka'ba in Makkah. Just as Jerusalem had held back the Quraysh, Ka'ba held back the Jews. These were some of the reasons that turned Jews gradually from indifference to hypocrisy, and, finally, to active opposition.

A third element also grew up in Madinah. It was the hypocrites. These were largely a disaffected people with political ambitions. They were led by 'Abdullah ibn Ubayy who, like the Quraysh in Makkah, could not tolerate the growth of Islam as another power in the region. But, unable to do anything about it, he and his followers outwardly professed Islam and waited to see who would emerge victorious: Islam or its enemies. They numbered many hundreds and at the time of every crisis sided with the enemies of Islam.

When the Prophet arrived in Madinah, almost the first thing he did after building a mosque was to institute brotherhood between the emigrants (*muhajirun*) and the Madinah muslims who were called helpers (*ansar*). Each *muhajir* was made a brother unto an *ansari*. They were to share their homes, wealth and property. They even inherited each other until the commandments came later abrogating all inheritance save by blood. In a world where people divided themselves into clans and tribes, with their loyalty only to their groups, in the right or wrong, and all not infrequently battling with each other over insignificant causes, this institution of brotherhood and its complete success was a remarkable achievement. For those who stared with wonder and disbelief it was a warning too that their strife torn structures would have little strength against the organizing and uniting power of Islam.

## COVENANTS

The next thing the Prophet did **was** to hold a census of the Muslim population in Madinah. Then he got the boundaries of the city that was to emerge from the dwellings marked. That done, he turned his attention to the tribes living around. He worked out various peace treaties with them. One of the treaties said:

"In the name of God, the Compassionate, the Merciful. This is a covenant given by Muhammad to the believers and Muslims of Quraysh, Yethrib, and those who followed them, joined them, and fought them. To the Jew who follows us belongs help and equality. He shall not be wronged nor shall his enemies be aided. The Jews shall contribute to the cost of war so long as they are fighting alongside the believers. The Jews of the Banu `Auf are one community with the believers. The Jews have their religion and Muslims have theirs ... piety and loyalty stand in the way of treachery ... None of them (the parties of the covenant) shall go out to war save with the permission of Muhammad, but he (or anyone) will not be prevented from taking revenge for a wound ... Each must help the other against one who attacks the people of this document ... The wronged must be helped ... This deed shall not protect the unjust and the sinner."

Thus, by the foregoing pact, the city, its property and human life were made inviolate. Crime was forbidden and unity among men and tribes established. It was a major achievement considering the anarchic era. The major Jewish tribes, Banu Qainuqa, Banu Nadir, and Banu Qurayda, had not joined until then. It was only smaller Jewish clans that had done so. But when they began to find how everyone was reaping prosperity out of peace, they too joined in to sign various pacts of non aggression, mutual help and cooperation with the Prophet and the new community.

## CALL TO THE JEWS AND CHRISTIANS

The treaties, however, had not been worked out with mere political ends in view. They were meant to create an atmosphere of peace and trust conducive to proper presentation and understanding of Islam. At Makkah the atmosphere of fear and discord was the singular reason for Islam's poor growth. Time was now ripe for serious discussions, although, as we shall see, just as the Quraysh of Makkah, the Jews of Madinah also failed to respond positively. They were led by people of small minds who could neither evaluate the truth that was dawning upon the land, nor were politically mature enough to assess the fast changing situation around them. It was particularly odd that the Jews, who were otherwise known for their shrewdness, acted stupidly on many occasions. They were always on the wrong step and always in alliance with the losing party. Although it cannot be denied that the odds were against them: had they made peace with the Prophet and allowed their masses free mix up with the Muslims, surely they would have lost them to Islam. Like all outdated and corrupted religions, they held their masses more by blackening other religions than by whitening their own.

The Qur'an addressed them at length, recounting their long history and drawing lessons that they should have learned over the centuries. But the revelations concerning them evoked only wonder at the Prophet's in depth knowledge of their history and hatred at being exposed by a non Israeli. Few came to Islam while the great majority remained solidly behind the rabbis, the priestly class. We present here only the opening verses of a long address to them.

*"Children of Israel*: (the address was to the rabbis and the form of address was meant to remind them of their noble origin: Israel being a Prophet of God), *remember those of My blessings with which I graced you* (such as raising Prophets among you) *and fulfil your promise unto Me* (that you will obey Me and My Messengers) *I shall* (thereupon) *fulfil My promise unto you* (of triumph over the infidels and Paradise in the hereafter). *And stand in awe of Me* (caring not for what people will say of you if you accept the new call). *Believe in that which I have* (now) *bestowed from on high which confirms what you have* (that is, the Torah) *and be not the first to deny it* (so as to set the precedence for those who will follow you), *and sell not My signs for a paltry gain* (that is, do not hide the facts about the new message from fear of people responding to it favorably and your losing you income that accrues to you through them) *but fear Me alone* (and not the circumstances of poverty). *And overlay not the truth with falsehood* (that is, do not offer an obscure interpretation of truth and falsehood so that the masses remain confused about Muhammad and his message) *and conceal not the truth while you know* (that it is the truth, even if revealed to a non

Israeli)" Chapter 2, Verses 40 44.

During the same early Madinan years, a delegation of the Christians of Najran arrived in Madinah. They were sixty riders led by three men, one of whom was a Bishop. They entered into discussions with the Prophet who offered them plain guidance against their complex beliefs that left them dissatisfied at their hearts. The Prophet told them to desist from their assertion that Jesus is the son of God and a third person of the Trinity. But they side tracked him into arguments that had no basis in reason or revelation. He told them at last: "Submit yourselves." They said, "We have submitted." He said, "You have not submitted, so submit." They replied, "Indeed we submitted before you." He said, "You lie. Your assertion that God has a son; your worship of the cross and your partaking of pork hold you back from submission." Taken by surprise, they asked in vexation. "But who is his father Muhammad." God then sent down a detailed account of Jesus. The opening verses said:

"*Alif. Lam. Mim: God, there is no god but He, the Living, the Self subsistent, the Eternal.*" (i.e. He transcends all that they have invented about Him, Who exists by Himself needing no second or third person to support Him. He is the Living One, unlike Jesus who was not, became, and then was no more) Chapter 3, verses 1 and 2.

And,

"*Verily in the sight of God the nature of Jesus is similar to the nature of Adam whom He created out of dust and said unto him: `Be', and he was.*" (Chapter 3, verse 59)

And,

"*Say* (unto them O Muhammad): `*O people of the Book! Come to a word common between us: that we shall worship none but God; that we shall associate not aught with Him; and that some of us shall not take others* (of our like) *as our lords besides God.'* *But if they turn away, tell* (them O Muhammad), `*Bear witness that we have surrendered*" Chapter 3, verse 64.

The truth is few of the Jewish and Christian masses are aware that their religion has no historical or rational basis. The authors of the Old Testament are anonymous. The origins of the first five books of the Pentateuch (the Torah, supposed to be revealed to Moses 1300 years before Christ) can only be traced, with great difficulty, so far back as between the 9th and 5th centuries before Jesus, and that those so called "original" documents have long perished. What is in hand now is translation of the translation. The masses are unaware that in the Bible there are defects "so many" and "so serious" (in the words of the foreword to the King James Version), that it has several times required revisions. (Even the Desert Storm Bible of 1991 was revised in four places!). The common people do not know that in the Holy Bible there are stupefying contradictions, pornography, erotic poetry, and even incest committed by the prophets in a state of drunkenness!

The Christians are generally unaware that the New Testament (the four Gospels) attributed to the Apostles of Jesus, were actually composed by unknown men about 70 to 150 years after Jesus in a language that Jesus did not speak; that the present four Gospels were chosen for canonization from dozens that were in current 300 years after Christ; that the founder of Christianity was not Christ, who said "I am sent but for the lost sheep of Israel" (Matthew, 15: 24), rather Saint Paul, who never saw Christ; that the word "Trinity" does not occur once in the Bible; and that today's "facts" of divinity and "sonship" of Jesus Christ were hotly contested by the earliest Christians and were finally incorporated into the Creedal Statement of the Church, despite protests by many, in the council of Nicaea in 325 C.E..

Finally, they are unaware that both the Gospels as well as the Old Testament predict the coming of the Final Prophet. Jesus is recorded in the Gospel as saying, "And I will pray the father, and He shall give you another comforter, that he may abide with you forever" (John 16: 7), and, "Nevertheless, I tell you the truth; it is expedient that I go away: for if I go not away, the comforter will not come unto you." (John 16: 12)

Nevertheless, the Jews also joined in the discussions that took a tripartite form. They disagreed both with the Prophet and the Christians. They refused to admit that Jesus was a messenger of God born of virgin Mary. They imputed impropriety to her in explaining Christ's miraculous birth. At one point the Prophet asked the Jews: "Do you believe that Jesus was (born of) God's word (of command)...His slave and His messenger?" They replied: "God forbid (that he be a prophet)." The Prophet then turned to the Christians and asked them the same question: "Do you believe that Jesus was God's slave and His messenger?" They replied, "God forbid that Jesus be His slave."[16]

The discussions proved futile and the Christian delegation returned to Najran. The Bishop however confided to his son later that he felt this was the true Prophet. To the astonished son he explained that having received from Rome honors and subsidies for construction of Churches, he could not betray them. The son, however, later embraced Islam, as did the people themselves of Najran who sent another delegation to the Prophet in the 9th year after *hijrah* to pledge Islam. On no occasion did a war take place between them and the Muslims.

## THE STATE AND ITS ANTAGONISTS

Meanwhile the style and nature of the Qur'anic revelations had changed. Laws concerning marriage, divorce, inheritance, crime, trade and commerce were revealed. Later, laws governing inter state relationships were dictated. The long awaited permission to retaliate force with force was also granted to the Muslims who had been restrained for 13 long years. The revelation concerning *Jihad* said:

"(Permission to retaliate is hereby granted) *To those on whom war has been imposed. For they have been wronged. And* (let them not be impressed by the might of the enemy, for) *Allah is Capable of helping them.* (This permission is for) *Those who have been expelled from their homes, in defiance of right,* (for no cause) *except that they say: `Allah is our Lord.' And, hadn't it been for Allah checking one set of people against another set, surely, many monasteries, churches, synagogues and mosques in which Allah's Name is recited much  would have been pulled down. And Allah shall surely help those who will help Him. Indeed He is Powerful, Mighty."* (22: 39)

16 *Safwah Al Tafasir* A. Sabuni Vol I, p 192.

Thus we see that gradually Madinah grew into a well organized state with the Prophet as its head. It was a new experiment in the long history of the anarchic Arabia and friend and foe alike watched the developments with interest. But not everyone viewed it as a healthy development. The Quraysh in Makkah and the Jews in Madinah could not let a powerful and vigorous state grow in their midst. The Quraysh decided to take the first step towards uprooting the new order. However, little did they realize that they were up against a genius, against whom they themselves were, despite all their sharp qualities, but little men. The Prophet broke them piece by piece, and destroyed them little by little, without any threat, without much violence and without his adversaries feeling any real decline in their power and influence. Every day that melted into the oblivion, the Quraysh lost some ground, but shrugged it off as a loss of useless stretch of desert. But, on a sudden, they found themselves at an abyss. Behind them was the Prophet, and ahead of them a steep fall. They had no choice but to turn back and accept him on their knees. The whole process  of the struggle between the Prophet and the Quraysh  is one of the most fascinating ones in history and deserves more research than a few dozen books that have appeared on the subject.

However, presently, they confiscated the property of the Muslims that had left Makkah, and banned their entry into the city. This was against all prevalent laws and a severe blow to the *muhajirun*. Some of them had brought from Makkah nothing but the clothes they had on. The Quraysh further let know the Madinans that if they would not throw out the Prophet they would have to face the Makkan rage.

They made it unsafe for the Muslims to move about in the country except in organized and armed bands. This had its effect on the economy of the Muslims. The generosity of the *ansar* notwithstanding, starvation set into Madinah.

In reply to their efforts to choke Islam, the Prophet began sending small bands of men who scouted the area around Madinah to give the impression, firstly, that the new state was well prepared to defend itself, and secondly, to warn the Quraysh that if they would not come to terms with the Muslims, allowing them to visit Makkah, granting them  freedom to preach in the tribes, and move about freely for trade and business, there was going to be no peace. These bands generally hovered around a passing trade caravan of the Quraysh, but avoided conflict. Since more than half the total trade of Makkah and Tayif with Syria was through a route that touched Madinah, the Quraysh were alarmed. But not unduly. They were too large and powerful to be disturbed by this minor irritation and seek to come to terms with the Muslims. They decided to rely on force. They increased the number of guards with each trade caravan and began to raid Muslim area. One such raiding party managed to carry away some Madinan cattle. Although the Prophet himself went out in pursuit the raiders managed to escape. Thus a state of war came to exist between the two and the Quraysh made no secret of their firm intention to destroy Islam and Muslims root and branch. They wrote letters to the Madinans to that effect. In such a situation it was only a question of time for the hostilities to begin.

## BADR

In the second year after *hijrah* the Prophet learnt that a large Makkan trade caravan was on its way back from Syria under the command of Abu Sufyan.[17] While preparations were underway in Madinah to attack the caravan in retaliation of the recent raid on Muslim cattle, Abu Sufyan got wind of the Madinan intentions through his agents and sent word to the Makkans of the possible Muslim attack. This was just the signal the Quraysh were awaiting. They swiftly raised a prized volunteer corps of over 900 well armed men with almost all able leaders and staunch enemies of Islam in its ranks and began to march towards Madinah.

The Prophet had set out with about 300 companions, and received news of the Makkan force on his way. But he was not sure

---

[17] It is reported that the caravan was carrying large amounts of arms, obviously for use against the Muslims. But this writer could not verify the authenticity of the report.

which of the two he would encounter first: the caravan, or the Makkan army. Nevertheless, he continued to march towards Makkah. Many Muslims were quite fearful because they knew that whether or not they encountered the caravan, they were sure to meet the Makkan army, facing which, they thought, would be calamitous since neither were they in sufficient numbers nor properly armed to meet an organized force of the sort advancing on them. The trade caravan in any case could not be encountered, for Abu Sufyan made his people travel two full nights, and one whole day allowing only a few hours of rest. He also changed the route leaving the Muslims much behind in vain pursuit.

The Muslims, however, continued to march until they reached Badr, a watering place about 150 km. from Madinah. By then they had learnt that Abu Sufyan's caravan had escaped and that the Makkan army was advancing towards them. The Prophet knew that it would take the Makkans about a week to reach Badr. Inexplicably he decided to advance to Badr, rather than retreat to the safe grounds of Madinah. The men under his command were, compared to the Makkans, in the ratio of 1:3. They were ill fed and inadequately armed. How poorly armed they were can be judged from the fact that later when actual fighting began, they started by pelting stones at the enemy. Moreover, many of them had not given their pledge to fight and so the Prophet had to seek their consent before deciding to enter into the conflict.

Another discouraging factor was that they were at a great distance from Madinah and no quick help could arrive from there. They had no beasts also to escape in the event of a defeat. It is reported that they had but a solitary horse. The number of camels was 70, that is, a camel for every 4 5 persons, while the beast cannot take more than two at a time. Finally, it was enemy territory, the tribes around were either allies of the Makkans or hostile to Islam. Perhaps the only way to explain the Prophet's decision to meet the Quraysh at Badr was that he might have received instructions from on High to do so. Otherwise militarily it was perhaps not the best thing to do.

It was only when the Makkan army arrived that the Muslims learned that they were facing no mean a force. All the tough warriors  many considered equivalent of tens and twenties were in the fore front. The Makkans on their side wondered what could prompt the Muslims to the impending suicide. Last minute efforts at peace were foiled by Abu Jahal and a tough battle ensued. But the wonder of wonders: Muslims emerged victorious. No less than 70 Makkans were slain, most of them the chiefs and renowned fighters, and as many captured to the loss of 13 Muslims.

Judging by statistics, it was a minor battle. But it proved to be a very significant one. The result changed the history of nations and destinies of billions of people. Without exaggeration, the battle can be considered "the most important" of all the battles and wars that human history has recorded in its annals. After the victory, when 70 Makkans were taken prisoners, and the Muslims were discussing what was to be done with them, the Prophet remembered 'Adiyy, his courage and his kindness in giving him the protection during his last days at Makkah. "By God," he said, "had 'Adiyy been alive today and requested their freedom, I would have set them free." The ultimate decision anyway was to release the prisoners on ransom. The ransom of those that knew how to read and write was to teach the art to 10 Muslims.[18]

## THE MURDER OF KA'B B. AL ASHRAF

In all, the Prophet either ordered, or gave his approval to, the killing of four of his enemies. The background story of each of them is different. We shall present the case of only one: Ka'b b. Al Ashraf, who was done away with after Badr.

When the Prophet sent an advance party to Madinah to give them the happy news of victory at Badr, one of those who wouldn't believe his ears was Ka'b. b. Al Ashraf. He was a rich Jew who lived in his own strong fort. He was a poet too. And a powerful one. When he heard the news of the death of Makkan chiefs, he said: "By God, those were the noblest of Arabs. If the news

[18] At least this writer does not know of a parallel case in history.

is true, then it's better to be dead than alive." Then he went to Makkah and receiving the hospitality of one of the chiefs began to say poetry mourning the death of the Arab chiefs and inciting the Makkans to revenge.

Now, the Arabs feared none as the poets. They were in that society what the press is today. Caught on the wrong foot, and satirized by a poet, a man in those days didn't have even the deserts to hide himself in shame, for a good piece of poetry reached every home, every tent, and every shepherd in the remotest of areas faster than the news of gold find. The poet could destroy a man more effectively than the sword could. And Ka'b was a powerful poet.

Therefore, the Muslim poet of Madinah Hassan b. Thabit, answered him with his own lampoons. Then a poetess entered the fray and Ka'b replied to her too. Finally, having cooled his anger a bit, and having succeeded in convincing the Makkans that the axe needed to be ground a little bit sharper for the next encounter, which couldn't be delayed too long, he returned to Madinah.

His conduct so far was deplorable, especially so since the Jews had entered into a peace pact with the Prophet, and, had Ashraf done that against any other tribe he would have met with his immediate end.

Nonetheless, he didn't stop at that. He began to compose poems attacking the honor of Muslim women. This was quite unacceptable to Arab honor. They wouldn't tolerate it in the pre Islamic days, and now with Islam giving their women an impenetrable shield from loose tongues, it sounded all the more insulting. Probably they restrained themselves because of the Prophet. Otherwise, in the normal course of things in Arabia of that time, Ashraf wouldn't have enjoyed many bright mornings.

Nevertheless, with the security offered by his own standing as a renowned poet, personal physical strength (which amounted to that of ten men), and his invincible fort, he was not simply saying terrible things, but composing poetry that was to be recited by hundreds and thousands of people in sitting rooms, street corners, pubs, and every such place where it would hurt and insult the Muslims.

Had he stopped at that, he would have still escaped punishment. But in his fanaticism and incurable hatred he went another step forward. He attacked the honor of two women Umm al Fadl and Umm Hakim, composing obscene lines that spoke of how one's hips worked, and how another bared herself in the nights for the pleasure of Ka'b and his pals: both women being no less than the aunts of the Prophet. Ka'b said:

Are you off without stopping in the valley
And leaving Umm al Fadl in Makkah?
Out would come what she bought from the peddler of bottles
Henna and hued dye.
What lies between her ankle and elbow is in motion (meaning the buttocks),
When she tries to stand and cannot.
Like Umm Hakim when she was with us
The link between us firm and not to be cut.
She is one of B.'Amir who bewitches the heart,
And if she wished she could cure my sickness.
The glory of the women and of a people is in their father,
A people held in honor true to their oath.
Never did I see the sun rise at night till I saw her
Display herself to us in the darkness of the night.

"Oh God," the Prophet said in total frustration, "deliver me from this son of Ashraf, howsoever You will."

In response, one night a group of Muslims advanced, with the Prophet's leave, to Ka'b's fort. They lured him out and killed him. It should be of interest to note that the men that had participated were all of the same tribe as Ka'b, the man who took the leading part had been suckled by the same nurse as he, and was, prior to his Islam, a great friend of Ka'b.

## EXPULSION OF BANU QAYNUQA'

The stunning defeat at Badr disturbed many, especially the Jews. They began to feel very unsafe, and decided to deal directly with the Muslims so as to break their power before they grew stronger. To start with, they began to create strife in Madinah by spreading rumors and re kindling the pre Islam hatred among the two leading tribes, Aws and Khazraj. Then they sent their delegates to Makkah to incite them to revenge. Their poets, apart from Ka'b b. Al Ashraf, used literary power  equivalent of modern day media power  to foment hatred. It was quite clear that they were preparing grounds for war with the Muslims despite the pact. One day a Muslim woman went to the markets of Banu Qainuqa seeking to remodel a piece of jewellery. She was persistently asked to unveil. She refused. A shopkeeper secretly tied the hem of her skirt to a peg so that when she stepped down the shop her body became exposed. The Jewish shopkeepers around let out a boisterous laughter. This enraged a Muslim passer by who killed the shopkeeper. In retaliation Jews from other shops came down and killed him. A general fight ensued but died down with intervention. The Prophet later reproached the Jews and invited them to Islam. Their arrogant reply was: "Muhammad! We are not the kind of people you met at Badr. We are fighters." These words were from the supposed allies! The Prophet laid siege to their forts. In two weeks time they surrendered and were expelled from Madinah.

## DEFEAT AT UHUD

Meanwhile the angry Quraysh were making large scale preparations for a revenge attack on Madinah. One or two attempts on the Prophet's life through their agents had failed. A kidnap attempt also floundered. In the year 3 A.H. they came down with an army of 3000 well equipped troops and headed for Madinah. They camped at Uhud, a mountain 5 km. north of Madinah. The Prophet intended to defend the town from within. But younger men insisted on going out and meeting the enemy in the open. 'Abdullah ibn Ubayy the arch hypocrite also advised against going out. But on the pressure of the majority the Prophet came out with a thousand men. A little out of town ibn Ubayy broke away with 300 of his followers saying that he had not been heard while the counsel of younger ones had been followed.[19] The Prophet continued to march with the remaining men.

[19] Some changed sides in the battlefield and killed Muslims through treachery.

Despite their numbers, the Quraysh had, as a safety measure, brought their women to discourage their men from running away from the battle filed. These women began to beat their drums and sing songs encouraging their fighters. When the Prophet heard them, he responded with the supplication: "O Allah. I seek Your Strength, and with You do I join. I fight in Your cause. Enough for me Allah, and a good Supporter is He".[20]

A fierce battle ensued. Initially, the Makkans suffered losses and began to flee. But due to a strategic mistake and disobedience of the Prophet the scales turned and the Muslims suffered defeat. Seventy of them were martyred, many by the friendly swords because of the confusion. The rest fled to Madinah and other places of hiding. Then the news spread that the Prophet had died. Many came back to fight and die, considering life worthless after the Prophet.

The Makkans concentrated on the Prophet and directed a heavy onslaught on his life. But despite several attempts lasting several hours by the best of their fighters, many of whom had sworn that they would not come back without his head, he escaped with merely four front teeth chipped off by a flying missile, and an unstoppable bleeding injury in the forehead. The remarkable valor of a couple of his followers, including, at least, one brave woman, Umm 'Ammarah, who formed a human shield around him taking the strikes against their bodies is history. They helped him climb a hill, made difficult because of the wounds, and the two heavy coats of mail he had put on that day. Once on the top, the Muslims threw rocks at the enemy to discourage them from advancing.

Abu Sufyan, the chief commander came to the foot of the hill and enquired if the Prophet was alive. When he didn't receive an answer he assumed that he was dead. Then he enquired about Abu Bakr and 'Umar, two of his very close Companions, and again the Prophet restrained them from answering. But when he shouted out "Glory to Hubal," a Makkan deity, then the Prophet could not sacrifice his mission against the risks to his life. He ordered 'Umar to answer: "God is Most High and

---

[20] *Tafsir Al Manar*, verse 122, *Surah Al 'Imran*.

Most Glorious. We are not equal. Our dead are in Paradise and yours in Hell."

The Makkans mutilated the bodies of the fallen Muslims. Their accompanying women wore necklaces made of earlobes and noses cut from the dead. Then the army began to march back. On the way they realized that they could have plundered Madinah. But just as they were pondering if they should turn back, they learned that the Prophet had gathered his forces and was coming in their pursuit. So they abandoned the idea. They didn't seem to be too sure of their victory. The Prophet pursued them to some distance and then returned to Madinah. In this battle he lost many dear ones including his brave uncle Hamza. To the end of his own life, he did not forget the martyrs of Uhud. He used to visit their graves every year. It is reported that in the last year of his life he visited their graves twice. The next notable event was the treachery of Bir Ma'una. This happened when the Prophet was requested to send some men who could teach Islam to the tribes of Najd. He sent 70 of his most learned followers. But they were deceived on the way and all but one were slain at a place called Bir Ma'una (the watering place of Ma'una).

## EXPULSION OF BANU NADIR

These events encouraged the Jews. They began to create troubles of all sorts. However, finding themselves weak against the Prophet, they relied more on inciting the Arab tribes to a general war, than their own valor. The Prophet, however, was desirous of renewing the pact with them   the earlier one having being so often violated. But when he visited them in their dwellings, they tried to kill him by dropping a rock over him while he was resting under a wall. He withdrew quickly and gave them 10 days to leave the city. They withdrew to their forts and began to make preparations for a showdown. They were promised help by the hypocrites of Madinah. A force of 200 was to come to their rescue immediately. But the help failed to materialize and after 20 days of siege they agreed to leave the dwellings with all their belongings. Singing, dancing, beating drums, and taunting Muslims they came out of their fort, went north to Khyber 200 km. from Madinah, and settled among the Jews of that place. That was in 4 A.H. It was however only the large and influential families of the Banu Nadir that had left. Independent families continued to live in Madinah peacefully. There were some of them that remained even till the reign of Umar, the second caliph of Islam.

Meanwhile Islam continued to grow. The Prophet had entered into treaties of friendship with various tribes within close range of Madinah. The people of these tribes lent their ears and many succumbed to Islam's appeal. The five time daily Prayers had already been declared obligatory, by now Ramadan fasts were also instituted and *zakah* (the welfare due) was being collected at the state level. Evils of all kind had been eradicated allowing only virtue and piety to flourish. The resultant peace within the new state and its surroundings was enviable. The change was obvious to anyone who came into Madinah. It was a spiritual oasis in the desert of empty souls. It was enough for a heathen to be given an opportunity to spend a few days in Madinah to convince him of the truth of Islam which was then not in books or sermons but in practice. In fact, those captured in battles were tied up in the mosque so that they could observe Islam from close range. They ended up embracing Islam.

## THE BATTLE OF THE TRENCH

The growing strength was obviously anathema to the Quraysh. The remaining Jews of Madinah also felt very uncomfortable. They realized that they would not be able to hold their masses for long from succumbing to the influences of Islam. Way up, the Jews of Khyber were also not to stay inactive. They began to incite the Makkans, the surrounding tribes and the hypocrites in Madinah to action and war. They also succeeded in persuading the large tribes of Ghatfan of central Hejaz to come out against the Prophet. It was strange that the believers in monotheism were working hand in hand with the pagans against the monotheists. Dr.Israel Wilfenson, himself a Jew, writes in his book, *The Jews in Arabia*: "By allying themselves with the pagans they (the Jews) were in fact fighting themselves contradicting the teaching of the Torah which commands them to avoid, repudiate   indeed to fight the pagans."[21]

21 *Rahmat e 'Alam*, Abul Hasan Ali Nadwi.

Their efforts in any case proved fruitful. In 5 A.H. a combined army of 10 12,000 troops marched towards Madinah. It seemed to be the pan Arabia decision to do away with the Prophet and his men. The advancing army was certainly large enough to finish off the Muslims in a couple of hours. But there was no panic in Madinah. Muslims began to make preparations to defend the city. Salman, a Persian convert suggested that trenches be dug around the city in places where natural fortification of forests or mountains did not exist. It was a massive job however. For in about 15 days a trench about 12 13 feet wide, 10 feet deep and 5 6 km long had to be dug. The allies, both Jewish and non Jewish, lent no help despite the treaties. To add to difficulties it was another year of drought. Nevertheless, every single hand, the Prophet included, was put to service. With stones tied to their stomachs in an effort to fight off hunger the Muslims applied themselves to the job feverishly and completed the trench just a day before the Makkan army arrived. The strategy, which was new to the Arabs, took the invaders by surprise. Nonetheless, they laid siege and made several attempts to cross the trench but failed. They lost several of their prized men in those attempts, one of which lasted for a whole day.

Nevertheless, their blockade caused starvation among the Muslims. The Jewish forts at the rear of Madinah had sufficient stocks of food grains. But for the Muslims, things worsened as the siege prolonged. In addition, another development became a cause of anxiety. The Prophet learned that the Jews of Banu Quraydah had set aside the treaty of friendship and were preparing to strike from the rear. Some Jews were sighted near the Muslim dwellings  either they were measuring the strength of the forces left in the town or were scheming to plunder it. One of the Jews was sighted climbing a wall and was struck down by a Muslim woman. The Prophet sent emissaries to assess the situation and get the peace pact renewed. But the Jews misbehaved with the delegates and gave clear indication of what they intended to do. The news of this development, however, was kept back from the masses for fear of panic.

At that stage the Prophet sued for peace and offered one half of the crops of Madinan dates for lifting of the siege. But the Makkans set impossible conditions and the siege continued. As luck would have it, some 20 camels loaded with food stuff and fodder sent by a Jew to the Makkan army fell into Muslim hands and for a couple of days they had enough to eat. Meanwhile disunity arose among the various invading tribes. One reason was the prolongation of the siege. Not only was it hard upon the impatient bedouins, but they were also facing depletion of their food stocks. The Prophet capitalized on these factors and sent a newly converted to spread doubts about the sincerity and steadfastness of the various partners of the coalition. Each was led to believe that the other was preparing to betray. The Jews too could not summon enough courage to strike from the rear. They wanted the Makkan army to storm in. But failure in earlier attempts had cautioned the Makkans, and so they wanted the Jews to strike first and divert the attention of the Muslims. This led to each suspecting the fidelity of the other. Finally winter storms set in. Madinan cold itself was harsh enough. Now winds began blowing at tornado speed. Tents and vessels were flying in all direction. Occasional rains also accompanied the winds lowering the temperatures to freezing point. Three stormy nights and days and the besieging army had had enough. First individuals, and then whole tribes packed up and departed. Finally the Quraysh had to also to call it a day and had to trek back to Makkah in not a very cheerful state.

The Prophet predicted, "This is the last time they came on us. Hereonwards we shall be on the offensive."

## THE BANU QURAYDAH

The Muslims returned to Madinah greatly relieved. But hardly had they laid down their weapons that the Prophet was ordered through revelation to attend to the Jewish menace. He laid siege to their forts. The Jews felt safe and strong. They had enough water and cultivable lands within the forts. In preparation of attack on the Muslims earlier during the siege, they had collected their animals in. They could, therefore, sustain the siege for months and years. But for some unknown reason they lost heart and gave up in 20 days. However they committed a mistake. Instead of submitting themselves to the judgement of the Prophet, who would have punished them, at worst, with no more than banishment, as in the case of the other two clans, the Banu Nadir and Banu Qaynuqa', they chose an old ally of theirs as the arbitrator. He was one of those who had visited them seeking peace during the Makkan siege. He had seen them both in times of peace as well as when the Muslim survival depended on how they would behave. He gave a decision that no one, not even the Jews themselves, thought as unjust for a people who had proven so treacherous: death for the men of fighting age and slavery for the rest. One of their leaders declared that the Jews were themselves to blame.[22]

After this, no fortified Jewish settlement remained in Madinah.

## THE TREATY OF HUDAYBIYYAH

The next year, that is, in 6 A.H., the Prophet started for Makkah with the intention of *umrah* (the lesser pilgrimage). He had 1500 followers with him. But the Makkans would not let them enter the city. The Prophet had no intention of war. He agreed to go back and perform the Abrahamic pilgrimage the next year if the Makkans would settle down to a compromise. Among the Makkans the conviction was gaining ground that they were not going to defeat Islam through force: at least it would not be as easy as they had originally thought. Therefore, they agreed to a 10 year peace treaty. The Prophet accepted almost all conditions set by the Makkans. Some conditions were considered humiliating by many Muslims who were very upset at what they thought was a show of weakness. They advised against

---

[22]The courage of a Jewish woman cannot go unrecorded. 'Ayesha, the Prophet's wife relates that a woman of the Quraydah clan was sitting with her talking and laughing immoderately while the men of the clan were being beheaded nearby. Then suddenly someone called out her name. 'Good heavens!" 'Ayesha jumped. 'What's the matter?' she asked. 'I am to be killed,' the woman said. 'And what for?' the terrified 'Ayesha enquired. 'Because of something I had done,' she replied. (She was killed for murdering a man called Khallad bin Suwayd with a millstone.)

signing such a treaty. But the Prophet went ahead despite the disapproval and even anger of most of his Companions, including a figure like 'Umar, and put his seal on the document. The major points were:

1. Muslims will go back that year and perform the pilgrimage only the next year.

2. Here onwards anyone of the Makkans who embraced Islam and joined the Muslims in Madinah would be returned to the Makkans, while those of the Muslims who will abandon Islam and join the Makkans would not be returned.

It so happened that just as the treaty was being discussed one such Makkan Muslim appeared, who was chained by his people because of his Islam. He also carried visible signs of torture on him. He pleaded that he be released and allowed to join the Muslims. The terms of the treaty had been written down but it wasn't signed yet. But the Makkans insisted that since the terms were agreed upon the man would not be released. To the dismay of his followers, the Prophet, in his eagerness for peace, allowed the man to be dragged back to Makkah, merely promising him that Allah will open a way for him.

The immediate advantage of the treaty, however disadvantageous it might have appeared at the time of its signing, was that the Muslims were now free to move in all parts of Arabia, including Makkah. This gave rise to free mixing of Muslims with non muslims at all levels. And as all conversations ultimately led to religious discussions, it became possible to present Islam to the masses who also had the opportunity now to see the Muslim life and behavior from close quarters. The result was that within one year after the treaty more people had accepted Islam than they had during all the preceding 20 years. This was what the Prophet had in mind when he had accepted the humiliating conditions of the treaty.

## KHYBER

A couple of months after the pact of Hudaibiyyah, the Prophet turned his attention to the recurring Jewish menace, now originating from Khyber. It will be remembered that it was they who had brought the Arab tribes upon Madinah. An emissary of some 20 men, including a couple of rabbis, had been despatched from Khyber to all parts of Arabia. At Makkah the Quraysh enquired: "Tell us O Jews. You are learned in the Scriptures. Which of the two is better guided: us or Muhammad?" They told him: "By God! You are better guided than he. You revere this House, feed the pilgrims, offer sacrifices to God, and worship your ancestral gods." From Makkah they went to the Banu Ghatfan promising them one year's Khyber crop if they would help the Quraysh. They had also visited Banu Sulaym, the Ahabish and others.

The Prophet marched on them two months after the treaty of Hudaibiyyah. He took with him only those that had accompanied him to Hudaibiyyah, ie., about 1400 men. The Khyberites came to know of the march through hypocrites of Madinah, and sent word to Banu Ghatfan to send help. They responded with an immediate contingent. But the Prophet misled them by taking the route that could lead him to the settlements of Banu Ghatfan in central Arabia. Fearing his attack on their tribes instead of Khyber, the contingent quickly returned to their settlements and the Prophet veered around to carry on to Khyber. On the way he again changed the route to arrive at the north of Khyber. This broke the morale of the Khyberites: for this meant the escape route to Syria in the north stood blocked.

The next day in the morning, when the Jews began to come out with their picks, shovels and flocks, they found the Muslim armies in front of them. They retreated and sealed their forts which numbered, all in all, big and small, about a dozen. The Prophet attacked the forts and took them one by one. One was well defended and several commanders failed to take it. Finally he gave the standard to 'Ali and told him: "Go (and attack) until God gives you victory. But first invite them to Islam. Tell them what is God's right on them. And remember that one man guided by you to Islam is better than a hundred prized camels." The fort was captured.

When the Jews saw their forts falling one after another, they applied for peace on condition that they be allowed to go to Syria. The Prophet agreed. Subsequently they came back and said that they be allowed to stay back and work on the farms that had been taken away from them and had been distributed among the Muslim soldiers. The Prophet agreed to that also on condition that if he wished to expel them he would have the right to do so.

When peace prevailed he was invited for a dinner by a Jewess. The roast lamb was poisoned. The Prophet felt it as soon he chewed a morsel and threw it out. But a Companion, who hadn't seen him reject it, continued eating and died. The Prophet also felt its effects on his body for many months. It seemed to have been a powerful poison. The woman confessed to the crime but for some reason the Prophet let her off unpunished.

## AN ACCOUNT OF THE PROPHET'S EMISSARY TO THE ROMANS

Between Hudaybiyyah (6 A.H.) and his death in the 10th year after *hijrah*, the Prophet sent emissaries to various kings and rulers of adjoining states. They were sent to al Yamama, al Bahrayn, Oman, Yemen, Alexandria, Persia, and the Roman ruler in Syria. The account of the Prophet's letter carried by Dihya Kalbi to Heraclius, the Roman emperor, makes interesting reading. The sources are Tabari and Bukhari, and the translation, in most part, that of Alfred Guillaume.

Ibn Shihab Zuhri says he heard from 'Ubaydullah b. 'Abdullah, who heard it from 'Abdullah b. 'Abbas to whom Abu Sufyan said: "We were a merchant people and the war between us and the Apostle had shut us in, until our goods were getting rotten. When there was an armistice between us we felt sure that we would be safe. So I went out with a number of Quraysh merchants to Syria making for Gazza. We got there when Heraclius had conquered the Persians who were in his territory and driven them out and recaptured from them his great cross which they had plundered. When he had thus got the better of them and heard that his cross had been recovered he came out from Hims, which was his headquarters, walking on foot in thanks to God for what He had restored to him, so that he could pray in the holy city.[23]

[23] The Cross was recovered from the Persians by Heraclius in 628 C.E. The Holy city referred to is Jerusalem.

Carpets were spread for him and aromatic herbs were thrown on them. When he came to Aelia and had finished praying there with his patricians and Roman nobles, he became sorrowful, turning his eyes to heaven. His patricians said, "You have become very sorrowful this morning. O King." He said, "Yes, in a vision of the night, I saw the kingdom of a circumcised man victorious." They said that they did not know a people who circumcised themselves except the Jews and they were under his sovereignty. They recommended him to send orders to everyone of authority in his dominions to behead every Jew and thus rid himself of his anxiety.

And by God as they were trying to induce him to do this, lo! the messenger of the governor of Basra came in, leading a man, while the princes were exchanging news, and said, "This man, O King, is from the Arabs, people of sheep and camels. He speaks of something wonderful that has happened in his country, so ask him about it." Accordingly the King asked his interpreter to inquire what had happened and the man said, "A man appeared among us alleging that he was a prophet. Some followed and believed him; others opposed him. Fights between them occurred in many places, and I left them thus." When he had given this news the King told them to strip him; they did so, and lo he was circumcised!

Heraclius said: "This, by God, is the vision I saw; not what you say. Give him his clothes. Be off with you." Then he summoned his chief of police and told him to turn Syria upside down until he brought him a man of the people of that man, meaning the Prophet. We were (that is, Abu Sufyan, the narrator) in Gazza when the chief of police came down upon us asking if we were of the people of this man in the Hejaz; and learning that we were, he told us to come to the King, and when we came to him he asked if we were of the clan of this man and which was the nearest of kin to him. I said that I was, and by God I have never seen a man whom I consider more shrewd than that uncircumcised man, meaning Heraclius. He told me to approach and sit in front of him with my companions behind me. Then he said, "I will interrogate him, and if he lies confute him," But, by God, if I were to lie they could not confute me. But I am a man of high birth too honorable to lie and I knew that it was only too easy for them, if I lied to him, to remember it against me and to repeat it in my name, so I did not lie to him.

The first thing Heraclius asked me was, "Tell me about this man who claims that he is a prophet. How is his lineage among you?"

I said: "He is of noble lineage."
Then he asked, "Has anyone of you made the same claim before?"
I said: "No!"
Then he asked: "Has he had a kingship in his family before?"
I said: "No!"
Then he asked: "His followers are noble people or the lowly?"
I said: "The lowly."
Then he asked: "His followers are increasing in number or decreasing?"
I said: "They are increasing."
Then he asked: "Is there anyone who has left his religion after acceptance due to hardships?"
I said: "No!"
Then he said: "And have you charged him with speaking a lie before he made this claim?"
I said: "No."
Then he asked: "Has he ever been treacherous?"
I said: "No! But just now we have worked out an armistice with him and we have to see what he will do with it." ("And", Abu Sufyan said, "this was the only unfavorable comment I could make before Heraclius").
Then he asked: "Have you been at war with him?"
I said: "Yes."
"What were the results?", he asked.
"Its fortunes have varied, sometimes we have won sometimes he," said I.
Then he asked me what he preached.

I said: "He says, "worship one God, join no partners unto Him and give up what your forefathers have taught you (idolatry)." He also tells us "to pray, speak the truth, be chaste, and show kindness to the kin."

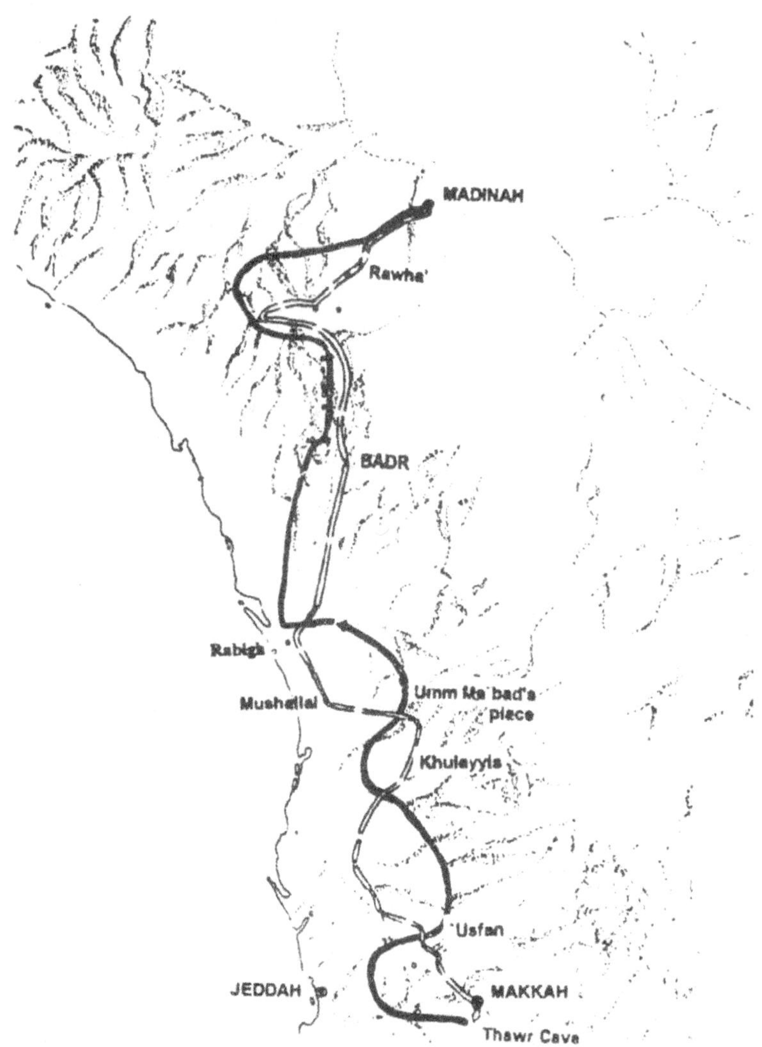



Map showing the route adopted by the Prophet in his hijrah journey. The discontinuos line shows the normal route between Makkah and Madinah (Yethrib). All along the Prophet had to conceal his identity. If recognized, he would have been captured and handed over to the Quraysh for a prize.

Letter of the Holy Prophet written to Munzir bin Sawa, the ruler of Al-Bahrayn, admonishing him and informing him that the Prophet has received good reports of him (and therefore expects him to respond well). Munzir embraced Islam upon receipt of the letter.

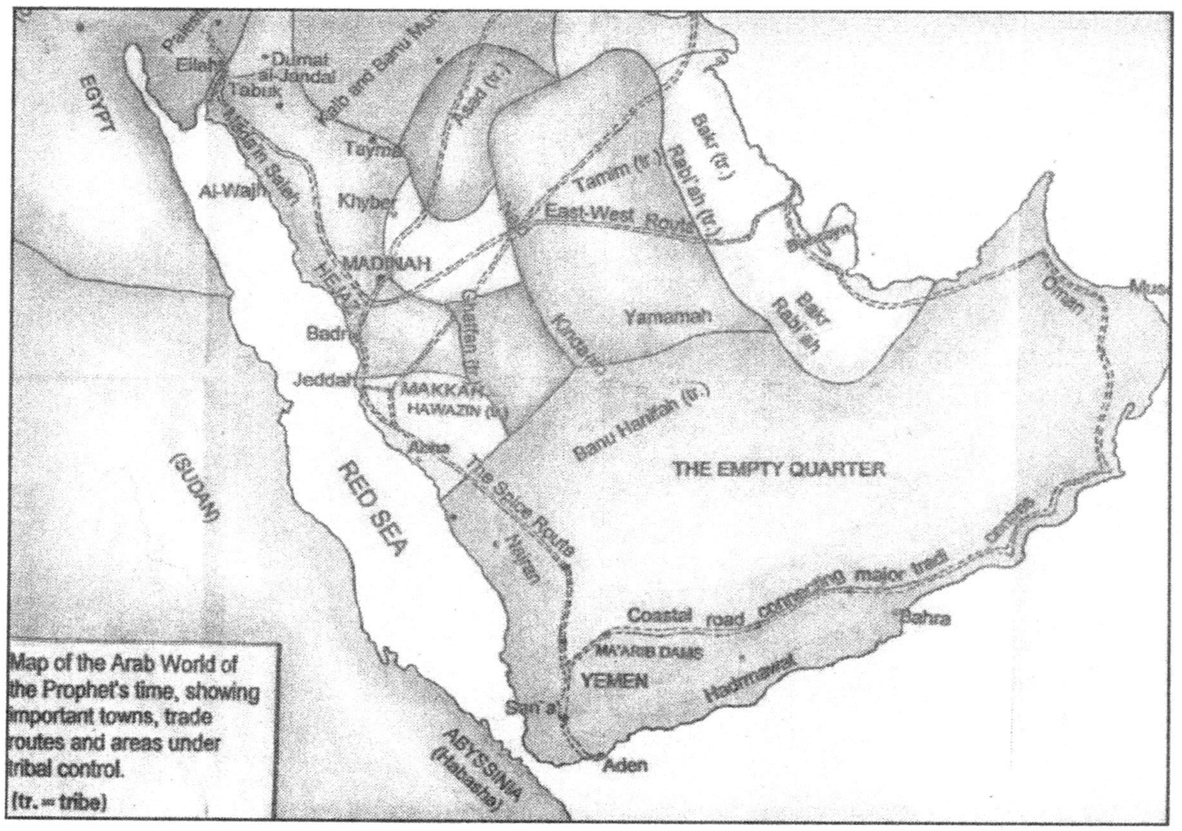



Map of the Arab World of the Prophet's time, showing important towns, trade routes and areas under tribal control. (tr. = tribe)

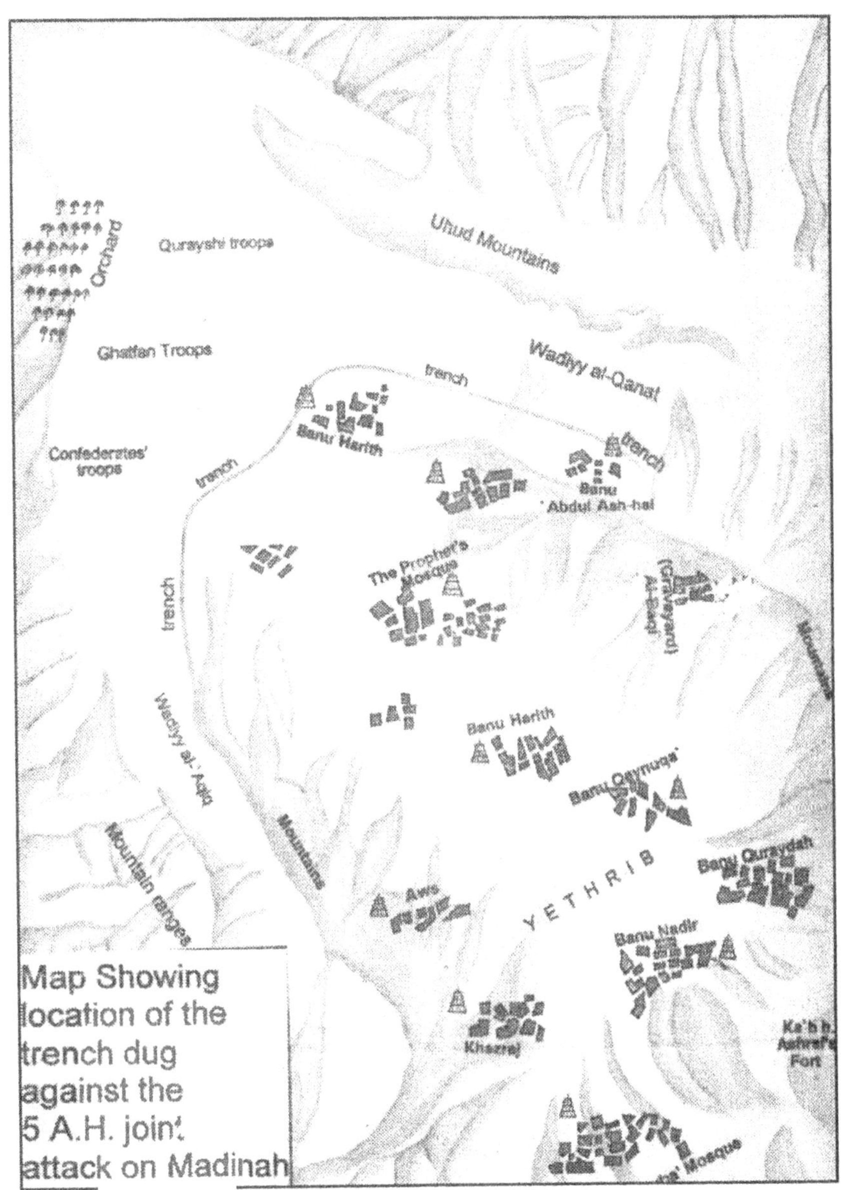


Map Showing location of the trench dug against the 5 A.H. joint attack on Madinah

Then Heraclius told his interpreter to tell us: "I asked you about his lineage and you said he is of pure and noble lineage; and I tell you God selects as a prophet only one of noble lineage. Then I asked you if anyone else had made the claim before, and you said no. And I said to myself, if anyone had made the claim I would have thought that he is imitating the previous one. Then I asked you if there had been a king in his ancestors and you said no. And I thought that if there had been a king in his ancestors he was trying to recover his sovereignty. Then I asked you if he ever lied before claiming prophethood and you said no. And I thought that a man who did not lie to men would not lie against God. Then I asked you if the noble follow him or the lowly. You said the lowly. And I tell you it is always the lowly who follow the prophets. Then I asked if their number was increasing or decreasing. You said they are increasing. And this is the case of the faith until it reaches its zenith. Then I asked if anyone left him due to hardships, and you said no. And I say this is the sweetness of faith. When it enters the heart it does not depart. Then I asked if he was treacherous. You said no. And that is how the Messengers are, they are never treacherous. And then I asked you what does he teach. You said, he asks you to worship One God, attributing no partners unto Him, and forbids you from worshipping idols and bids you to pray, be honest, chaste and kind to the kin. And I tell you if what you say is true then soon his will be the ground under my feet now. Indeed I knew that a prophet was expected but I did not imagine he could be one of you. If I could reach him, surely I would wash his feet."

Then, (Abu Sufyan continues), Heraclius asked to be presented the letter of the Prophet that Dihya al Kalbi had brought to the Governor of Basra who had sent it to Heraclius. Heraclius read out the letter. It said:

"In the name of Allah, the Compassionate, the Merciful. From Muhammad the slave and prophet of God to the Emperor of Rome. Peace be upon those who follow the guidance.

"I invite you to accept Islam. If you will accept Islam you will be saved and God will give you a ten fold reward. But if you will reject then upon you will be the sin of the Aristin.[24] And

---

[24] It could mean both the Roman subjects or the followers of Arius who were struggling to restore faith in the unity of God in place of the Church sanctioned Trinity.

'O people of the Book. Come now to a word common between us, that we serve none but God, and that we associate not aught with Him, and take not some of us as Lords apart from Allah. And if they will turn their backs, say: Bear witness that we are Muslims.'"

'Then', Abu Sufyan said, 'A tumult arose in the court and they were sent out."

## THE FALL OF MAKKAH

Two years after the treaty of Hudaibiyyah the Makkans violated it. In retaliation the Prophet marched to Makkah with 10,000 followers. The Makkans were much surprised. The Prophet's ranks seemed to have swollen ten fold in two years since Hudaibiyyah. As against that their own ranks had depleted. Most of their leaders had either been slain in battles or had converted to Islam. They offered no resistance to the three pronged entry of the Muslim army into Makkah. The chiefs of the Quraysh who had persecuted the Muslims for ten years and faced them in battles after battles for another ten, and had on numerous occasions tried to get the Prophet assassinated were at his mercy now. "Well! What do you expect me to do with you?" the Prophet asked them when they had been assembled before him. "You are a noble brother, son of a noble brother. We expect good from you," was the reply. "Go! You are free," the Prophet declared.

Then he entered the Ka'ba, broke all the hundreds of idols that adorned the House, and got the pictures of Mary and Jesus that adorned the inner walls of the Ka'ba obliterated. As he came out he was saying: "All praise be to Allah Who kept His promise, Who helped His slave (ie. the Prophet himself), and Who defeated the armies all by Himself." Then Bilal, who once used to be dragged in the streets of Makkah, was ordered to climb up the Ka'bah and make the prayer call. When he cried: "God is great," and "I witness that there is no god save (One) God," a Makkan quipped that he was glad the Makkan chiefs were not alive anymore to hear this black slave crying out like that from the roof of the Ka'bah.

Later the Prophet sent scouts to all parts of Makkah and surrounding areas to destroy idols.

# HUNAYN AND TAYIF

A little later thousands of the adjoining tribes of Hawazin rose up against the Prophet and met him in a fierce battle in Hunayn. The Muslim were routed in the early stages and began to flee, but the courage of the Prophet who remained in the battle field with a handful of followers, encouraged them to return. And final victory was theirs.

Some of the tribes, especially those of the Tayif, fled back to the town and shut its gates. To break their power and complete his victory, the Prophet besieged the hill station. But, despite 20 days of tight siege, he could not subdue its inhabitants and so lifted the siege.

The Hawazin had brought all their women, children and cattle with them, in order to impress on their men that if they lost, all would be lost. The "back to the wall" strategy of course didn't work. And with defeat they fell into Muslim hands. By the prevalent laws all was booty, but the Prophet managed through a strategy to get the men, women and children released. The cattle was divided. The Prophet decided to divide the spoils among the Makkans, although it was the neo Muslims of Makkah who had fled the battle field first, causing panic. But if one reason was to retain them in Islam, necessary because the Prophet's own influence on the making of good Muslims of them would be a factor removed with his departure to Madinah, and perhaps also because he would have thought that the carrying away of the best of the cattle to Madinah would impoverish the Makkan region. Finally, he wanted to impress on his true followers that jihad was not booty collection.

Whatever the reason, not all Madinans were too happy about the decision. After all, weren't they the ones who had rallied behind the Prophet in the battle when others had fled? In fact a comment to the effect was also heard that "When it comes to offering life and limbs it is us who are called, but at the time of division of spoils, it is the Prophet's relatives who are remembered." When this comment reached the Prophet's ears, he asked the leader of the *ansar*, Sa`d b. `Ubadah, who had brought the comment to him, "Where do you stand, Sa`d." The upright man admitted he was with his men. The Prophet ordered the *ansar* to assemble before him. When they had gathered their chiefs, elders and all  and after Praises to God, he addressed them  thus:

"Tell me, O *ansar*. Is it not true that you were misguided and Allah guided you (through me)? You were poor and Allah enriched you through me? You were divided and Allah united you through me?"

"Why don't you answer me, O *ansar*?"

What answer could they have? So they said, "How shall we answer you, O Messenger of God? Indeed, Allah and His Messenger are most kind, and most generous."

"No, by God," continued the Prophet, "Had you wished you could have said  and you would be speaking the truth  that, 'You came to us discredited and we believed in you; deserted, and we helped you; a fugitive and we sheltered you, poor and we comforted you!" (Had you said that, you would have been speaking the truth).

"Are you, O *ansar*", he continued, "disturbed in your heart that I use the dregs of the world to win over people, while I entrust you to Islam?"

And then he added, "O *ansar*, are you not satisfied that the people should take away camels and goats with them, and you the Apostle of God with you?!"

The powerful words had their effect. There was not one of them whose beard was not wet with tears. "We are satisfied with the Apostle of God as our portion and our lot," they cried out in  unison.

The Prophet then left the assembly.

After a few weeks the Prophet went back to Madinah. There he received the news that the Romans were gathering a huge army to invade Madinah. He announced his intention to face up to the challenge and march to Tabuk, a place 800 km north of Madinah. It was not the right time though. The crops in Madinah were near ready for harvesting; the Muslims were feeling both the economic as well as the physical strains of previous excursions; and this year's summer was exceptionally hot. But no excuse was accepted. Every able man was to go. Hypocrites came in continuous streams presenting false reasons and requesting permission to be left behind. The Prophet allowed them to stay back.[25] Some of them accompanied and created various problems on the way. No true Muslim was allowed to remain behind. After the hectic preparation of a week or so the Prophet set off with 15,000 men. The journey proved to be strenuous and they reached Tabuk in 22 days, hungry and thirsty. Sometimes a dozen men chewed a single date in turns. Many hypocrites fell back on the way. And those remaining were reminding the Muslims of the dangers ahead: "Do you think that fighting the whites is going to be the same as Arabs against Arabs? By God, we can see you fleeing into the mountains tomorrow to save your lives."

At Tabuk the Prophet addressed them on more than one occasion. On one occasion he leaned against a tree trunk and told them: "Should I not tell you about the best of the people and the worst of the people? The best of the people is he who goes into the way of Allah on the back of his horse, or camel, or on his feet, (and continues) until death overtakes him. And the worst of the people is that audacious man who reads the Qur'an but pays no attention to its demands."

The Romans, however, impressed by the courage of the Prophet, dispersed and no fighting took place. The Prophet sent troops to surrounding areas to subdue the tribes. In two weeks time they were on the same trail, marching home with perhaps no material gains. But the Muslims demonstrated such discipline, dedication to God and His religion, and such inner strength that perhaps gave the Prophet's successors, the courage to venture the struggle against the two mighty giants of the time: Romans and Persians.

[25] One of the hypocrites Jadd b. Qays, gave an interesting reason for staying back. When the Prophet asked him if he would be accompanying him he said: "You know I have a weakness for women. I'm afraid I will not be able to resist myself if I see Roman women, so let me stay back."

During the return journey some hypocrites again attempted at the Prophet's life but failed. The Prophet recognized them as they approached him in the darkness of the night but took no action against them afterwards. Meanwhile, those of the hypocrites who had stayed behind in Madinah constructed a mosque in his absence and began to use it as their headquarters to plan their actions. The Prophet destroyed it after his return.

The 9th year is called the year of deputations. Arabs were so far waiting to see which of the two, Islam or Quraysh, would emerge triumphant. With the fall of Makkah and destruction of the age old idols, tribes after tribes sent deputations to Madinah to pledge allegiance to Islam.

## THE FAREWELL PILGRIMAGE

In the 10th year the Prophet went to Makkah to perform pilgrimage purely in the Islamic form known as *hajj*. There was not a single non Muslim now in Makkah. Excerpts of the Prophet's sermon on the Mount of Rahmah (in 'Arafat) addressed to over 100,000 piligrims are as follows:

"All praise be to Allah. We glorify Him and seek His help and pardon; and we turn to Him. We take refuge with Allah from the evils of ourselves and from the evil consequences of our deeds. There is none to lead him astray whom Allah guides aright, and there is none to guide him aright whom He leads astray. I bear witness that there is no God but Allah alone; having no partner with Him, and I bear witness that Muhammad is his bondman and His messenger. I admonish you, O bondmen of Allah, to fear Allah and I urge you to His obedience and I open the speech with that which is good!

"Ye people! Listen to my words: I will deliver a message to you, for I know not whether, after this year, I shall ever be amongst you here again. O people! Verily your blood, your property and your honor are sacred and inviolable until you appear before your Lord, as this day and this month is sacred for all. Verily you will meet your Lord and you will be held answerable for your actions.

"Have I not conveyed the message? O Allah! Be my witness.

"He who has any trust with him should restore it to the person who deposited it with him.

"Beware, no one committing a crime is responsible for it but himself. Neither the son is responsible for the crime of his father, nor is the father responsible for the crime of his son.

"O People! Listen to my words and understand them. You must know that a Muslim is the brother of another Muslim and they form one brotherhood. Nothing of his brother is lawful for a Muslim except what he himself allows willingly. So you should not oppress one another.

"O Allah! Have I not conveyed the message?

"Behold! All practices of paganism and ignorance are now under my feet. The blood revenges of the days of Ignorance are remitted. The first claim on blood I abolish is that of Ibn Rabi`ah Ibn al Harith who was nursed in the tribe of Sa`d and whom the Hudhayl killed.

"Usury is forbidden, but you will be entitled to recover your principal. Do not wrong and you shall not be wronged. Allah has decreed that there should be no usury and I make a beginning by remitting the amount of interest which `Abbas b. `Abd al Mutallib (the Prophets's uncle) has to receive. Verily it is remitted entirely.

"O People! Fear Allah concerning women. Verily you have taken them on the security of Allah and have made their persons lawful unto you by words of Allah! Verily you have got certain rights over your women and your women have certain rights over you. It is incumbent upon them to honor their conjugal rights and not to commit acts of impropriety which, if they do, you have authority to chastise them, yet not severely. If your wives refrain from impropriety and are faithful to you, clothe and feed them suitably.

"Behold! Lay injunctions upon women but kindly.

"O People! Listen and obey, though a mangled Abyssinian slave be your *amir*, if he executes (the ordinance of) the Book of Allah among you.

"O People! Verily Allah has ordained to every man the share
of his inheritance. The child belongs to the marriage bed and
the violator of wedlock shall be stoned. He who attributes his
ancestry to other than his father or claims his clientship to
other than his masters, the curse of Allah, that of the angels
and of the people be upon him. Allah will accept from him neither
repentance nor righteousness.

"O People! Verily Satan is disappointed of ever being worshipped
in this land of yours, but if he can be obeyed in anything short
of worship he will be pleased in matters you may be disposed
to think of little account, so beware of him in your matters
of religion.

"Verily, I have left amongst you the Book of Allah and the Sunnah
(practices) of His Apostle which if you hold fast, you shall never
go astray.

"And, if you were asked about me, what will you say?"
The people replied: "We bear witness that you have conveyed
the message and discharged your ministry."

## DEATH

Early in the 11th year after *hijrah*, the Prophet visited the
cemetery of the town in the middle of the night. He prayed
there for the dead. The following morning he was too ill to leave
the bed and appointed Abu Bakr to lead in Prayers. When he
recovered a little after a couple of days he went to the mosque
and addressed the people: "Has he not made the right choice,
who, when given the option of this world, the other world, or
accepting simply what is with God, chooses the last alternative?"
He was of course referring to himself. He also instructed the
emigrants during the speech to treat the *ansar* well, who he
feared would soon dwindle in numbers. The same day he was
very ill again and a few days later he breathed his last. His
last act was to give away in charity a few Dinars he had in
his possession, saying he would not like to meet his Lord with
that on him. And the last words he spoke were: "Nay, but the
exalted companion in the Heaven."

# THE REACTION

His followers could not come around to accepting that he was dead, or that a prophet could die. The shock was so great that even a man like 'Umar drew his sword and threatened to kill anyone who would say he was dead. Some thought he was visiting his Lord and would return soon. They were in this state when Abu Bakr arrived. He went straight to the body, uncovered the face, kissed it and said: "How beautiful you are, both dead and alive." Then he headed for the mosque where the people sat in tense disbelief. He went up the pulpit and when the voices had died down said: "People! Those who worshipped Muhammad may know that he is dead. While those who worshipped God may know that He is alive and never dies." Then he recited the following verse of the Quran:

*"Muhammad is but a prophet before whom many prophets have come and gone. Should he die or be killed, will you abjure your faith? Know that whoever abjures his faith will cause no harm to God, but God will surely reward those who are grateful to Him."*
(Chapter 3, Verse 144)

His followers shook away the shock of his death and rose up from the stupor, drunkenness and debauchery of centuries, to reach the borders of the two super powers of the time, the Byzantine and the Persian: with the flag of Islam held firm in their hands. In just over a decade they had destroyed them and replaced them with a spiritual empire that lasts to this day, proving the Prophet's prediction true that: "Soon you will battle the armies of Rome. You will emerge victorious and there will be no Emperor of Rome after that. And soon you will battle the armies of Persia. You will emerge victorious and there will be no Emperor of Persia after that."

# WIVES AND CHILDREN

## WIVES

The Prophet married several women. His first marriage was to Khadijah, a woman who proved to be of an outstanding character. Of course she had no difficulty in accepting her husband as a prophet since she, more than anyone else, had observed him in all circumstances of life. But credit must be given to her for the moral and material support she extended through and through of their 25 years of life together. Consequently she was one of those whom the Prophet respected, and loved. He held fond memories of her all his life. Many years after her death, in Madinah, he continued to send gifts to her friends. He used to mention her so often that once 'Ayesha felt irked and said something to the effect that she saw no point in recalling the memory of an old woman who had lost her teeth. The Prophet expressed his displeasure at the remark.

When she died, she left the Prophet passing through a very difficult time of his mission. Opposition to what he had brought was at its zenith. He didn't even have the right to preach within Makkah. With her gone, he had lost a staunch supporter and believer in his cause. Not only did he miss a supporter, comforter and a friend, he missed also the mother of his children. He had to fill the vacant house, even if he could not his vacant heart. He married Sauda, a woman in her fifties. He chose her perhaps because of her age and for the fact that she had lost her husband in Habasha during her stay there when she had migrated there accompanying the first batch. Those were a lot for whom the Prophet had a soft corner in his heart. He did not forget them at any moment of rejoice, and was very much pleased when in the sixth year after *hijrah*, they joined him in Madinah.

Sauda, however, had returned to Makkah earlier. Later, in Makkah itself, the Prophet married another girl, the only virgin that he married. This was 'Ayesha, just six years old at the time of the engagement. She was the daughter of the first

Muslim and a beloved child hood friend Abu Bakr. She did not enter his household until she was nine. This marriage seemingly served no immediate purpose. But it proved to be the most fruitful later. For 'Ayesha grew into a lady of exceptionally rich intellectual qualities, who looked at every aspect of the Prophet's private and public life with a keen eye, and related those details that were essential for the later legalists to work out the Law.

The next lady the Prophet took into marriage was Hafsa, the 27 year old daughter of his most powerful supporter after his uncle Hamza, and the second caliph after him, 'Umar ibn al Khattab. She had lost her husband at Badr and 'Umar had failed to find a suitable match for her. The Prophet rescued her.

Another lady that the Prophet married was the widow of another of his Companions, 'Ubaydah b. al Harith. He was sent with 'Ali and Hamza to face three of the challenging Quraysh in duel at Badr. 'Ali and Hamza slew their opponents but 'Ubaida received a serious wound. When he was picked up and brought to the Prophet, he placed his chin on the Prophet's foot and asked if he would be considered a martyr. He died a few minutes later. The Prophet married his widow. Her name was Zaynab bint Khuzaymah, and this was her third marriage. But she died within a few months.

The next lady that he married was Umm Salamah. She had once migrated to Abyssinia with her husband Abu Salamah. There they received false news of the acceptance of Islam by the Quraysh and returned. Back in Makkah they again became the target of brutal persecution. They decided to get away to Madinah. But hardly was the couple with its single child out of town, when the Makkans separated Umm Salamah and her child from Abu Salamah, saying he didn't have them with him when he had entered Makkah several years earlier. Undeterred, Abu Salamah continued the journey. A few months later, Umm Salamah managed to join him. At Badr, Abu Salamah received a large wound. He recovered from it but at Uhud he was struck at the same spot. The Prophet visited him at his house after the battle. To his great grief, he died in front of him. He had special regards for him and offered special burial prayers for him. Some time later he sent word to his widow that he desired to take her into wedlock. She politely refused when she answered that, "She suffered from jealousy (*ghirah*), was quite old, and had little children who would bother him." He replied: "As for your jealousy, Allah will cure it, as for your age, I am not very young either, and as for the children, they belong to Allah and His Messenger."

The next woman was married to him by Allah Most High Himself. She was Zaynab bint Jahash, previously married to Zayd, freed slave and adopted son of the Prophet. Their marriage had been arranged by the Prophet himself eight years ago in Makkah. But the pair didn't go well. And despite the Prophet's best efforts, Zayd divorced her. God Most High ordered him to marry her in order to emphasize the validity of a canon law that adopted sons do not become real sons, as in most other religions and cultures, and that there is no taboo on Muslims marrying former wives of their adopted sons.

Another lady that came in his wedlock was Umm Habibah whose circumstance of marriage will be presented in the next chapter. She too joined him in Madinah only three or four years prior to his death.

The Prophet married three more women. One was Juwairiyyah who was taken prisoner in a battle, but the Prophet married her. The result was that a whole clan comprising of over a hundred families that had been taken slaves was redeemed by the owners because they could not bear to keep any member of that clan as slave which was related to the Prophet. It is strongly suspected that he had married her for this reason. Another lady he married was Safyah, the former wife of a Jewish chief Kinanah, slain because the treasures of Banu Nadir were too dear to him. When captured after the battle, the Prophet asked him where he hid it. Kinanah expressed complete ignorance. The Prophet asked him if he was prepared to die if it was found that he had knowledge of it. He said yes. It was found in his premises and he was executed. (He was also ordered killed because he had killed a Companion of the Prophet). His wife Safyah was taken prisoner, but the Prophet married and then redeemed her. Another lady whom he married was Maymunah bint al Harith a 27 year old widow. He married her when he was in Makkah to perform *'umrah* in the 7th year after *hijrah*. 'Abbas, the Prophet's uncle, had suggested the alliance, perhaps to strengthen the family ties and win some Makkan families to the cause of Islam. The Prophet complied and requested the Makkans that he be allowed to extend his stay in order that he could arrange his marriage feast (*walimah*). They refused and insisted he leave the city within the three days he had been allowed.

Actually, he had those nine wives together only at the end of his life, since he married a few more in his late years. Nonetheless, there was nothing extra ordinary in his life with them. He had divided his days among them and used to spend a day with them in turns. Since they did not have children, save for those who had from previous marriages, and life was simple in those days, there wasn't much for them to do. They lived in separate apartments   hutments would probably be the right word   which, even by the prevalent standards, were poorly furnished. In fact, they were so poor that on important occasions they borrowed other women's jewelry to adorn themselves. After Khyber, their share of yearly provision used to be handed over to them at the beginning of the year. The allowance itself was meagre, and with the generosity with which they treated their guests, neighbors and beggars, they were soon short of the essentials. For a couple of years they bore it with patience. But when they saw war spoils arriving into Madinah regularly, and the common people benefitting from them, then their own poverty began to pinch them harder. They began to complain. When the Prophet paid no attention they surrounded him one day refusing to release him without promises of increase in their allowances. He was irritated by their behavior and on God's command gave them the option that they could stay with him under the same conditions, or part company, in which case he would send them away with gifts. All of them chose to stay with him, and the subject of provision was not broached again. The result was what 'Ayesha described later: "Full three moons would pass without our oven getting  lit."

However, it shouldn't be imagined that they were unhappy with him. Far from that. They were a lot that were submitted to God. When they knew that He wanted them to remain in that state of wants and shortages, they accepted it as the best thing imaginable for them. They placed their desires where they would adorn them most: under their feet. That explains why, even after the death of their husband they did not alter the style of their life. 'Ayesha, for instance, after the Prophet, once gave away huge amounts of money and materials that had been gifted to her by the Caliph of the time, before the evening would set, and broke her fast with dates and water.

The Prophet, of course, otherwise took care of them. He would tell them stories and listened to their innocent gossip. As 'Ayesha describes it, "He used to chat with us (for long hours), but as soon as he heard the Prayer call he would behave as if he didn't know us." One of them  chosen by the lot  always accompanied him in his journeys. In one journey he asked his Companions to go ahead a little. When some distance was made he invited 'Ayesha to race with him. 'Ayesha was then thin and lean. She won the race. Some years later, during another campaign, he invited her for a rematch. She had put up weight during those years. She lost the race. "This is the reply to the previous one," he told her teasingly.

## CHILDREN

Except for Khadijah none of his wives bore him children. By Khadijah he had two or three male children all of whom died in infancy. He also had 4 daughters through her, three of whom grew to womanhood, were married but died before him. The fourth was married to 'Ali and gave birth to the famous Hassan and Hussain.

A male child was also born to him through his solitary slave Mariyah who had been gifted to him by the Christian Governor of Egypt. The child, named Ibrahim, also died in infancy. The Prophet could not control his tears as he lifted the dead child. When someone expressed astonishment at his tears he said in effect: "The eyes are filled with tears and the heart is heavy with sadness. But the tongue will not say anything but what pleases the Lord."

# Chapter 4

# A SKETCH OF THE PROPHET'S CHARACTER

## THE PROPHET AS A PERSON

What has been stated so far can be described more appropriately as the birth, rise and triumph of Islam rather than the description of the life of its prophet. True, the struggle to establish Islam was the dominant feature of his life. But certainly, apart from a prophet, he was a human being too. He had his own personality, his own character, likes and dislikes, joys and sorrows. He was, all at once, a son, a father, a husband, a neighbor, a friend, a host, a guest, a trader, commander, guide, statesman, and a nation builder. In all these capacities he led his own personal life while he worked for his mission. And no doubt a student of his life would be interested to know how he led his personal life. However, in trying to portray his personal life, we face a difficulty. The Islam that he established is not simply a creed. It is also a code of conduct for the entire life. And what good is that code which cannot withstand the test of application? The Prophet therefore strove to demonstrate in everyday life the practicability of what he preached. So that, when 'Ayesha was once asked to describe his conduct she asked: "Have you not read the Qur'an?" In consequence the prophetic mission and his personal life are interwoven and co mingled in such complexity that it is not easy to separate one from the other. This requires that the whole of his life be studied and the student carry out the exercise himself of separating the human from the apostolic acts. This of course is not an easy task. Nonetheless, it must be attempted. For the more one can understand the Prophet as a human being, the more he is likely to appreciate his greatness and feel persuaded to follow his examples. It is for this reason that the Qur'an repeatedly asserts the essentially human nature of the Prophet the only difference being that he received revelations. It is to emphasize this fact that certain incidents occurred in his life that left no doubt about the human nature of his being.

Incidents such as, to mention just two, a brief spell of magic on him, and, the gradual reduction in the number of daily Prayers granted upon repeated requests during the night journey and ascent to the heavens (*al isra' wa al mi'raj*). The point, however, is that a serious student must attempt to study the whole of his life since what he was and what he brought are one and the same.

We shall, on our part, contend ourselves with the presentation of a general sketch of his character. This, if for the reasons of interest on the one hand, then to give this work some resemblance of a biography on the other. Although we must add in haste that even a schematic drawing or a set of slides of a modern complex city will say more about it than any short description will of the Prophet's character. All the same, here are a few lines.

## GENERAL APPEARANCE

A Bedouin woman who saw him during his brief stop over at her place in the company of Abu Bakr and a guide, while they were heading towards Madinah during their hijrah journey, described him to her husband in the following words. The grandiloquence, and the manner in which she comes back to what she has already stated, using different terms during repetition, is characteristic of a bedouin's talk and perhaps the result of an excited impression on a simple but observing mind. Other accounts suggest however that the woman did not stray far from the truth in her eloquent description.

"Of chaste appearance, bright faced, proportionately built: neither the stomach bulging out nor the hair falling. Comely face, elegant structure. Eyes black, tresses long and thick. Deep toned voice, long and glistening neck, sparkling pupils, thin (and grafted) brows, black curled hair. Dignified when quiet and graceful when speaking.

"Lovely and heart winning disposition from afar and sweet and charming from close. Words melodious and spoken with clarity. Sentences with neither too many words nor too few: the whole speech as like a lace of beads.

"Of medium height  so as not to look mean to the eyes glancing
down, nor too tall for the rising gaze to detest. A lovely fresh
branch (of a green tree), a graceful figure. Companions such
as those who hover around: who listen with patience when
he speaks and rush to carry out his orders.
"Served. Obeyed. Loved. Neither given to ill talk nor talkative
(himself)."[26]

## MANNERS

His contemporaries are in agreement that he was a man of
simple but elegant manners. His tastes were refined but he
never acted superior to others. When a Bedouin went to see
him but was too awe struck to be able to speak, he told him:
'Fear not! I am not an angel. I was born of a Qurayshi woman
who ate dried meat.' He had no difficulty, therefore, in attending
to his personal works. He stitched his shoes, patched his clothes
and milked his goat. He could squat on the ground in any vacant
place upon entering an assembly and would refuse to accept
a place of honor. He didn't like the people to stand up for him
when he entered their company. He wouldn't even allow them
to be following him in the rear. He preferred to keep himself
behind everyone when walking in a group. When camping in
the deserts he divided work and despite the protests of his
followers allotted some work to himself.

Simple he was and simplicity he approved of. And although,
he did not approve of his followers indulging too much in the
world, he disapproved of asceticism also. A young man came
to him and said: "You know O Apostle of Allah, I'm the most
handsome man of my tribe. I love to wear the best of clothes
and the best of shoes. Is that pride?" In reply, he gave pride
the definition that cannot be improved. "That is not pride,"
he said, "Pride is that you oppose the truth and look down upon
the people (with disdain)."

He mixed well with the people, passing a remark or two to
keep the conversation going and lending his smile when
required, but never laughing out boisterously. He had a good

[26] *Zad al Ma'ad*, Ibn Qayyim, vol.3 p.55.

sense of humor but disapproved of ungraceful tomfoolery. Predominant, however, was a thoughtful mood.

When he met a man, he treated him with respect. He never snubbed anybody and did not pass an unsavory remark about anyone behind him. Indeed rarely did he speak of a person behind him, unless it was to say something good of him. When he shook hands he never, as a gesture of good will, withdrew his hand first. When he spoke he turned to the man full, listened to him with attention and did not interrupt unless it was something against God and His religion. He never made signs with the eyes. Once a man, who had murdered a couple of Muslims, came up to him seeking his pardon. He wanted the man to be executed in retaliation, so he delayed pardoning him hoping that someone would come forward and kill him. But when that didn't happen, he pardoned him, since it was not his habit to turn down a request. Later he mentioned this to his followers  that he had delayed pardoning him in the hope that someone would kill him. They said they would have done that had he signaled with his eyes. "A Prophet does not signal with his eyes," he replied.

He kept himself, his clothes and his environment clean saying cleanliness is part of faith. Once he removed his not so dirty a shirt and asked 'Ayesha to wash it. She said she had done it just the other day. He said he was asking her to to do  it again because a clean cloth sings praises of God and ceases when dirty.[27]

In colors he preferred white and disliked red. He wore almost anything that would cover his body. Once he was spotted with a Yemeni pinkish garment in a moonlit night. The man who spotted him looked a fair amount of time at him and at the moon and concluded that he was more beautiful than the moon. But rich clothes he disdained. Once he put on a striped stuff. But after the Prayers he cast it away saying that it had distracted his attention in the Prayers. When he put on a new pair of clothes, he thanked God for bestowing him with what would

---

[27] *Al Durr al Mansur Fi Tafsir Bi al Ma'thur* by Jalaluddin Al Suyuti, Chapter 17, verse 44.

cover his nakedness, seeking for the good that it might carry and seeking refuge from any evil that it might conceal.

He wore shoes and cobbled them himself when the need arose. Following the Arab custom, he wore a turban, perhaps on important occasions, for we know that he oiled his hair and combed it quite regularly. He also applied antimony to his eyes. He brushed his teeth rather too often made from a fibrous fresh branch of a tree. When he smiled his teeth shined white. In brief, he kept himself neat and tidy saying: "Allah is beautiful and loves the beautiful."

Simple he was in his food habits too. He ate almost anything presented to him, except for what a man of good taste would reject, but reserved his remarks when he didn't like a thing, allowing others to relish. Meat and cold water he liked best. Sweet water used to be brought for him from a spring some five miles off Madinah since nearby wells yielded brackish water. Dates he recommended as regular diet especially for pregnant women. But garlic, onion and the like he turned away saying they emitted foul smell.

Of perfumes he was particularly fond. He was also fond of two more things: women and Prayers, as he himself stated once. But while we can explain his fondness for Prayers by citing his very regular habit of spending the best part of the night standing before his Lord until his feet swelled, we have nothing that can fix the exact meaning of what he meant when he said he was fond of women. It cannot surely be fondness of the kind that we all understand. The mere fact of him marrying several women does not support such a meaning. For if fondness of the kind that we all understand was a motive then surely the choices of wives were in several cases obviously wrong. Again, although he married several women, he did it very late in his life, and he didn't spend much time with them. In fact, statistics reveal that he spent the best part of his later life journeying. Finally, nobody marries several women and then lets them starve. Perhaps his statement about his fondness of women must be understood in the light of those scores of remarks that he made in order to restore women's rights in a society which accorded them a very low status.

He was quite fond of armor also and had several swords , coat of mail and other things in his possession. He also liked fast horses and camels.

He loved his Companions to the extreme degree. He said about himself and them: "My example is like that of a man who lit a fire. When it lit the surroundings, insects began to fall into it. He tries to prevent them but they overcome him and keep falling into it. I am holding you by your waists while you are falling into the fire." When he was told something uncomplimentary about his Companions, he said: "Don't speak to me about them behind them. When I meet them, I wish to meet them with a clean heart." When he went on a campaign, and announced that everybody was to participate, he was saddened to find someone he loved not in the company, fearing on his behalf that he might have stayed back with the hypocrites. Once during a campaign, Abu Dharr fell back because of a bad camel. Some people began to say that the man must be a hypocrite to have fallen back like that. But, later when they saw dust rising behind them, indicating someone was following them, the Prophet said: "Be it Abu Dhar!" As the figure neared, the Prophet was one of those anxiously watching as to who would emerge. He was pleased with what would please them, and saddened with what would sadden them. He knew the living conditions of most of them and waited for an opportunity to help them out. When he received goods, he would reserve things for those not present, and then, when the man appeared, he would say, "Here. Take it. I had hidden it for you."

When someone died and he was not called for his funeral, he was upset. In such an event he would make it a point to visit his grave and say prayers. He had announced that if anyone died leaving wealth, it was for his inheritors. But if he left debts, it would be upon him to repay. Obviously, he took a great risk when he said that. But those were days of an honest people. Nobody borrowed to leave it for the Prophet to pay. In fact, he loved them even as they lay in their graves. When one of his dear ones died, he married his widow, if he found that nobody was rescuing her from her ordeal.

Obviously, his Companions responded to him in like manner.

Once when he disappeared from sight, in days when attempts were being made to kidnap him, one of his Companions was so panic stricken that he crawled, fox like, through a drainage hole, across into an orchard, instead of using the gate, to check if he was there. On one occasion when someone presented himself with a golden ring in his hand, he removed his ring and threw it away, disapproving that men wear gold. When he had left people reminded the man to pick up his ring. The man said he was not going to take back what the Prophet had thrown away. 'Ali did not exaggerate when he said that to his Companions he was dearer than a glass of water on a hot day.

When he criticized them, he did it without hurting their sentiments. He never named people in his criticisms. Rather, he would say, "What's wrong with the people that they do such and such a thing," although it would have been a single person who would have done it.

He respected women a lot. Once an old woman detained him in the street for so long that it surprised a visitor. It was generally believed by his Companions that the freedom that his wives enjoyed had emboldened their women who were frequently citing the example of his wives while demanding their rights. Once when he advised something to a woman, she asked him if it was in the light of revelation he had received, or was it his own opinion. When he said it was his personal opinion, she said she wasn't inclined to accept it. "That's up to you," he told her.

Whatever he did, he did it well and recommended the same to others. He also advised persistence and steadfastness saying: Allah prefers the "less but consistent" over the "more but inconsistent." He set the example himself. For instance, one of his Companions says the Prophet smiled when he met him the first time. After that it did not happen, the Companion says, that he presented himself and the Prophet did not greet him with a smile. The example of his night vigils (*tahajjud*) can also be cited. He did not, until he had breathed his last, give up rising in the stillness of the night to offer his long Prayers: a practice he had adopted in Makkah 23 years ago.

Again, he was a hard working man and liked those who were

so. Once while shaking hands when he felt a man's hand unusually rough he asked him the reason. The man said he labored with them. He bent down and kissed them. In Makkah when he once returned from a tiresome day of preaching, during which he was ridiculed, jeered at and had dust thrown at him, he was told that a trade caravan had encamped outside the city. He started off immediately in order to present Islam to them. He was dissuaded from going especially as he appeared so weary. After all, he could wait until the morning. But his reply was: 'Who knows, I may not be alive tomorrow. Or they'll move away!'

On another occasion in Madinah at a time when rumors of Makkan invasion were rife and people slept with arms under their pillows, a loud uproar was heard in the night. People rushed out with swords in their hands. One group reached the outskirts of the city to investigate what was happening. As they stood there the clack trap of an approaching horse were heard. When the lanterns were raised, it was the Prophet. He said, in effect: "Nothing to worry. I have gone around the whole town and found nothing!" He was then about 55 years old. Ayesha was asked after him if he ever Prayed sitting. 'Yes' she said, 'when you had broken his back!'

## HONESTY

In his dealings with other people he was frank, straight forward and honest. His honesty indeed was of such order that even his worst adversaries   both of his times as well as of today have not questioned it.[28] Far from mincing words or making equivocal statements   a kind of lying perfected to excellence in our times   the Prophet disapproved of even making signs with the eye. When he spoke to a man he turned to him full

---

[28] By his adversaries of today we mean the Orientalists. However artful they may have been in their writings, anyone acquainted with their works must conclude that as a whole they have been at loggerheads with the Prophet. And the irony is that while they admit of his unquestionable honesty, they, in their efforts to block Islam's entry into the West have never hesitated to be dishonest.

so that his feelings could be read in his face. Even when joking he remained close to truth. This of course made it very easy for people to deal with him. For they knew that when he said a thing he meant it. If he said for instance to a man who had persecuted him for 20 years, and would not have hesitated to kill him a moment earlier, that he was forgiven, the man knew he was forgiven.

## GENEROSITY

The next thing best known of him is his generosity. 'Upper hand is better than the lower,' is his saying. When someone gave him a gift he found a way to return with something better. Early one morning in Makkah, a trade caravan encamped outside the city.

The Prophet visited the fair, chose a camel and led it away saying he would send the price. After he was gone, the trader began to worry about his money. A lady of the caravan said: 'Don't worry. I have seen the man's face. It was bright as full moon. Such a man will not deceive you. If he does, I will pay you the price.' By evening, the Prophet sent the money, and more: dinner for the trader!

In a journey 'Umar's son 'Abdullah was riding a fast camel which repeatedly overtook the Prophet's. 'Umar would not approve of it and would poke his son on the side signalling him to pull back his beast. But after a while the camel would overtake the Prophet's camel again which would again provoke 'Umar to use his stick. The Prophet watched the two with amusement. Then he asked if the camel could be sold  he was fond of good beasts. 'Umar said it was a gift. The Prophet refused. They agreed on a price. (Probably it didn't bother 'Umar if the camel overtook the Prophet's). However, when they entered Madinah, he paid the price to 'Abdullah. But when he was offered the camel he said: 'You can keep it. It is a gift.'

His generosity was almost legendary so that people did not hesitate at all to make importunate demands. And he gave them whatever he had. When he could not, he promised to give them when he would have something. It so happened that a man appealed for help. He told him that just then he did not have anything but that if he checked in again maybe he would have something to offer. 'Umar, who was present and knew how bold some people were in asking, could not restrain himself. He said: "But that you don't have anything just now absolves you of the responsibility, doesn't it?" At this another person quipped: "Keep giving, O Prophet, and fear not. The Lord in the heaven will not leave you in want." The Prophet was pleased with the remark.

Once he asked Abu Dhar if he could see the mount Uhud yonder there. Abu Dhar says he turned to look at the sun in the sky to gauge if he could return before sunset if the Prophet sent him to Uhud on an errand. Then he said, "Yes I can see the mountain." The Prophet said: "By God, if I had gold equal to this mountain, I would not like to have anything in my possession by the third day."

Once a Bedouin came to him and said very harshly, 'Muhammad! Goods (and materials) are neither yours nor your father's. Get loaded my camels with provisions." The Prophet got his two camels loaded with dates, barley and other things. On another occasion during a journey some Bedouins came to know that he was to pass by. When he arrived they encircled him and demanded to be given something. A tussle followed during which they pulled away his cloak. Somewhat confused, he took refuge behind a tree saying: "Give back my cloak. By God, if there were as many camels here as the leaves of these trees, I would give them all to you. You will not find me miserly, a liar, or unmanly."

But, despite his generosity, he used to say: "I am only the treasurer and the distributor. It is God who gives."

What could then be the result of such generosity but prolonged poverty. For he had no regular means of income. Weeks and months passed by and his oven was not lit. Sometime he would enter his house and ask, "Would there be anything to eat?" When told no, he would say cheerfully, "Alright. Let's call it a day of fasting," and he would fast for the rest of the day. The day he entered Makkah, leading his 10,000 followers, his dinner was bread dipped into a mixture of water and dried vinegar.

Once he was seen lying in the mosque turning from side to side due to hunger. Hunger in fact was so recurring that even his patient wives encircled him once and would not let him go if he would not promise to increase their allowances.

Once a Persian Companion invited him for a meal. He said he would go but 'Ayesha would be with him. The Persian would not accept the condition and went away. He came back however to repeat his invitation. The Prophet repeated his condition. Only the third time did the Companion accept them both. The historians explain that if the Prophet insisted on 'Ayesha accompanying him it was because just as he, she too had not had a square meal for many days; and the Companion initially refused because he could not afford dinner for both.

His generosity extended beyond material bestowals. He was generous with people also. He forgave the worst of his enemies those who had humiliated him before large assemblies  upon asking. In some cases it looked as if a pretext was being awaited for him to forgive. His generosity in fact went beyond this. Just as he was ever prepared for reconciliation with his adversaries, he strove to achieve the same between individuals and peoples. For instance, if he knew anything good could be said about a man or a people he did it in order to create an atmosphere of love and understanding. He knew of prejudices that people bear for each other and worked against them in a way that they remain effective even to this day.  The following sayings are  few examples.

About the people of Yemen he said: "Faith comes from Yemen." About the Egyptians he said: "Treat them well, for your mother was of them."[29]

About Syria he said: "Blessed be Syria. Allah's angels have spread their wings over it." About the Persians he said that from them a man would emerge who will bring down knowledge even if it were to be in Pleiades. In another version he said that if religious knowledge was to be in Pleiades, some people

---

[29] He was referring to Isma'il's mother Hajirah who was from Egypt. The Arabs are the descendants of Isma'il.

from Persia would bring it down. And, he is reported to have turned in the direction of the Indian sub continent and said that he could smell the fragrance of faith originating from there.

## HUMOR

As pointed out earlier, he had a good sense of humor. He jested with his wives, teased them and told them stories. But he stayed close to truth. When he asked a suitor what he possessed to present as dower to the woman he wanted to marry, the man said: "Nothing, except for the trousers I am wearing." He told him: "If you give away your trousers to her, you will be left with no trousers." When an old woman asked him to pray to God that she may be granted Paradise, he said: "Old women will not enter Paradise." Then he hurried to explain to the terrified woman that what he meant was that women would enter Paradise young. And when a woman came to him and said in her simplicity that her husband had invited him for a meal, without saying who her husband was, he asked: "Is your husband the man with whiteness in his eyes?" The woman was perplexed and remonstrated that her husband had no such defect. What the Prophet meant was simply the whiteness of the eye ball. And again, once when he was eating dates in a company he threw his seeds before `Ali. When they were finished he remarked: "You have eaten a lot of dates!" "Surely, but I didn't eat my seeds," was the lively answer.

Although his presence normally had sobering effect on the company, it was also known that a good joke would not be frowned upon. The following story will illustrate this well.

Abu Bakr had gone to Basra in connection with trade along with Nu'ayman and Suwaybit, two other Companions of the Prophet who had participated at Badr. One of them, Nu'ayman, was known for his sense of humor and practical jokes. One day when they were encamped outside of Basra, Nu'ayman asked Suwaybit, who was in charge of the provisions, to let him have his dinner. Suwaybit suggested they wait until Abu Bakr returned when they could share the meal. Nu'ayman was infuriated. He got up in a huff and went to another group of merchants to ask if they were interested in purchasing a slave. When they said yes, he explained to them that they may have some problem bringing him under control. He is a somewhat nutty boy, he told them, who may for instance, would argue that he is a free man and so on. They'll of course pay no attention to what he says until the fellow reconciles himself to their ownership. They agreed. The deal was struck for 10 camels, and they came to take Suwaybit away. Suwaybit of course vigorously protested that he was no slave, very much a free man and so forth. But who would listen? They put a rope around his neck and led him away.

When Abu Bakr arrived he was dismayed to learn of the matter. Frantically he followed their trail, caught up with them, returned them their camels and brought back Suwaybit.

When the story was narrated in Madinah in the presence of the Prophet, he also laughed along with others.

## CHIVALRY AND MAGNANIMITY

His marriage to Umm Habibah is a fine example of his chivalry. Daughter of Abu Sufyan the staunch antagonist of the Prophet, she had entered Islam in its early days. She had also to migrate to Abyssinia along with her husband to escape persecution despite the fact that she was the daughter of a leader of Quraysh. Such was the frenzy against Islam then. In Abyssinia however, her husband turned Christian. They were separated and Umm Habibah was left destitute with a child in a land where, as Asma', her companion later described, each day was spent in fear of life. She could not return to the parents of the kind she had: Abu Sufyan and Hind. Hind was the woman who had chewed Hamza's heart at Uhud. When the Prophet, who was then in Madinah, learned of her plight, he sent word for her hand. The offer pleased even the king of the country, Najashi, who himself performed the matrimonial ceremony. Thus Umm Habibah became his wife while her father was leading the Makkans against the Prophet, in all their battles after Badr. It was he who had inflicted the terrible defeat on Muslims at Uhud. But, on hearing of how the Prophet came to his daughter's rescue, even he was moved and the remark: "He is the honorable one who can not be put to blush," escaped him. And, moved by the Prophet's magnanimity he offered his second daughter's hand to the Prophet after his entry into Islam, but the Prophet turned down the offer saying that it was not permissible in Islam to take two sisters in wedlock at one time.

The case of the Persians in Yemen is another example of his magnanimity. The story is as follows: Just a few years after the birth of the Prophet, an eminent Yemeni, Abu Murra, was sent to seek help, either from the Romans or the Persians, to overthrow the tyrannous rule of the Abyssinians over Yemen. Abu Murra managed to reach the Persian Emperor Chosroes. He agreed to help. But what he did was to send 800 of those convicts who were awaiting execution on various counts in Persian jails. They were led by a fighter and a nobleman Wahriz. Fighting alongside the Yemenis, the Persians initially won. But later they were routed. So they applied to their Emperor for reinforcements. Chosroes responded with a force of 4000. In time these overthrew the Abyssinians and became the rulers of Yemen themselves. When the Prophet announced his office, Chosroes wrote to Bazan, the then Persian ruler of Yemen: "I am to learn that a man of the Quraysh has appeared in Makkah claiming that he is a Prophet. Go to him and ask him to withdraw. If he does, good. If he does not, send me his head!"

Bazan chose to be prudent and sent, instead, the Emperor's letter to the Prophet. In reply the Prophet told his emissary that the Emperor would be killed on such and such a day. Bazan of course was between amusement and uncertainty. He chose, however, to wait before taking some action. The prophecy did come true and he received news from Persia that Chosroes's son Shirawayh had assassinated his father. Bazan embraced Islam along with his countrymen in Yemen. But a problem arose. In the chaotic world of those times in which people divided themselves into tribes and clans, and where no one was secure unless of a powerful tribe or allied to one, the Persians got worried over their reduced status   now that they were rulers no more. Their messenger therefore asked the Prophet: "To whom do we belong?" The magnanimous reply was: "You are of us and related to us   the people of the House (of the Prophet)!"

# INTELLIGENCE

He had shown this gift very early in Makkah when the Quraysh rebuilding the Ka'ba came to disagree over who should put the Black Stone in its place. It was a matter of great honor and there was not a tribe that was not prepared to offer some lives for it if its claim was disregarded. A bloody conflict seemed inevitable. It was avoided when someone suggested that the first man entering the holy precincts the next day be appointed the arbiter. As chance would have it, it was Muhammad  not yet a Prophet  who appeared first. They were very pleased to see him coming in as he was known among them as the "trustworthy". The Prophet settled the issue in an intelligent manner. He asked for a sheet of cloth over which the holy stone was placed. Then all the tribal chiefs were asked to lift the sheet. When it was raised to the height he himself put it in its place.

At Badr, Muslims were able to capture two men of the Quraysh who had been sent to look for water. They were brought to the Prophet who tried to extract information from them about the strength of the Makkan army. But they gave contradictory and confusing answers. The Prophet got his answer in another way. He asked them how many camels were slaughtered every day. They said nine or ten. The Prophet told his Companions that the enemy numbered 900 to 1000.

After the defeat at Uhud the remnants of the Muslim force that had not fled to Madinah took refuge on a hill top. When the Makkans pursued them they rolled down stones and rocks on them. So they abandoned them and marched back to their tents some distance away. Now the tormenting question in everyone's mind was whether the Makkans were going to plunder Madinah or would they spare it. The Prophet sent 'Ali to follow them secretly and report back to him alone the manner of their journey, whether they rode their horses and led the camels or rode their camels and led the horses. What the Prophet reasoned was that if they rode their horses and led their camels it meant a short journey  and only Madinah could be the destination. But if they mounted their camels it would mean the journey was long and that Madinah was spared. 'Ali brought the news that they were riding their camels and leading their horses.[30]

The following story is another example of his intelligence. A man went to the Prophet complaining of persistent ill treatment at the hands of his neighbor. The Prophet told him to move his belongings to the street and sit there. The man carried out the instructions. Whenever some one passed by and enquired why he was sitting there, the man gave him the whole story of how he was ill treated and so on. Generally, the passer by sent a curse in the direction of his neighbor's house before moving on. Soon his neighbor was out begging him to move back on promises of good behavior.

## FORGIVENESS

When Hind b. Abi Hala was asked to describe the Prophet, among other things he said: "He was a kind man and not of harsh nature. He never insulted anyone...He got angry only when someone opposed the truth (of Islam) which he upheld vigorously. Otherwise he was never angry for personal reasons, nor did he seek revenge (on personal account)."

We might mention here the case of Abu Jahal's son 'Ikrimah. Abu Jahal's hatred of the Prophet knew no bounds. Distributed among a hundred men it could cause them all ulcer. He was the one who had foiled the last minute attempt at peace in Badr. It was he who had shed the first blood in Islam when he killed Sumaiyyah, a slave woman, at Makkah. And it was he who used to insult the Prophet in public  an intolerable thing for the Arabs even of this day. A man who was witness to a scene says he saw the Prophet going around the markets of Dhu 'l Majaz saying: "People! Say, 'There is no god but (One) Allah', and you shall flourish." Behind him was Abu Jahal throwing dust at the Prophet and yelling: "Let not this man's words deceive you into renegading your (ancestral) religion. (Beware!) he wants you to give up your deities Lat and 'Uzza!" The narrator says the Prophet paid no attention to Abu Jahal

[30] The Makkan intention could not have been gauged from the direction of their travel since both Madinah and Makkah lie to the south of Uhud.

and carried on with his task. And, in hatred of the Prophet and his cause, 'Ikrimah was the true son of his father. At the battle of Uhud, he was one of the three commanders. So when Makkah was subdued he slipped away knowing that the Muslims had orders to kill him even if found holding the Ka'aba covering. He was embarking a ship when someone who recognized him, assured him that the Prophet accepted the repentant, and that he could go back without fear if he chose to. When he presented himself to the Prophet he was so pleased that in his joyous surge to meet 'Ikrimah he did not notice that his cloak had fallen off his shoulders.

Then we have the case of Hind. She was the wife of Abu Sufyan, and daughter of another arch enemy of Islam, 'Utba. 'Utba had been slain at Badr by Hamza and Hind swore that she would eat his heart. At Uhud she brought a great marksman Wahshi with her to fulfil her oath. The man, who otherwise took no part in the battle, waited for Hamza to come into range. When he appeared he threw his javelin at him. The poisonous javelin hit Hamza in the stomach and he died immediately. Wahshi left the field and Hind set herself to the task of cutting open Hamza's chest. She took out the heart, chewed it but could not swallow it. The Prophet was extremely aggrieved. Hamza was his uncle and very dear to him. He was also a pillar of strength for Islam. When he entered Madinah he heard the voices of some women wailing for their dead. Tears filled his eyes and he said in grief: "But there is no one weeping for Hamza." When Makkah was subdued Wahshi also presented himself to declare his faith in Islam. The Prophet accepted his allegiance and forgave him.

When the Prophet sat at Mount Safa in Makkah accepting allegiance for Islam from groups of Makkan men and women, Hind also joined the women's ranks.[31]

---

[31] Hind in fact was lucky to be alive that day. For in Uhud, the Prophet gave his sword to Abu Dujanah and sent him into the battle field. Abu Dujanah struck a few down. But once when he was about to bring down his sword on a vanquished one, he realized that it was a woman. He wasn't willing to kill a woman, and, not at least, with the sword of the Prophet, and therefore, he spared her.

The Prophet first took the oath from men. Then he addressed the women. But each time he said something Hind interrupted him. His address and her interruptions went as follows. Notice also the woman's buffoonery and the Prophet's total seriousness:

The Prophet: "Pledge me your word that you will associate none with God."
Hind: "By God you ask us what you did not ask the men."
The Prophet: "And you will not steal."
Hind: (perhaps inadvertently), "Sometimes I take some money from Abu Sufyan's pocket. I do not know if that is lawful or not." (Abu Sufyan, who was also present spoke out: `So far as the past is concerned I make it lawful').
The Prophet: "So you are Hind daughter of `Utba." (He had not recognized her since she was veiled).
Hind : "Forgive me my past sins and God will forgive you yours."
The Prophet: "And you will not commit adultery."
Hind: "Does any decent woman commit adultery O Apostle of God?"
The Prophet: "And you will not kill your children."
Hind: "Well. We tendered them when they were young. When they grew up, you slew them at Badr. Now it's between you and them. (`Umar, laughed out wholesomely at this)."
The Prophet: "And you will not invent slanderous tales."
Hind: "By God! slander is a disgraceful thing. But sometimes it is good to ignore it."
The Prophet: "And you will not disobey me."
Hind: "Only in good things!"
The Prophet turned to 'Umar and said: "Take pledge from these women and seek Allah's forgiveness for their sins. Verily, Allah is Forgiving, Kind."
Hind was so impressed by his conduct that she said: "O apostle of God! No tent was more hateful to me than yours. But today no tent is dearer to me than yours."

## JUSTICE

An *ansari* was ordered by the Prophet to pay back to another man the debt he owed of dates. The *ansari* obeyed him but did not gave back the quality he had borrowed. The man refused to accept. The *ansari* exclaimed: "Do you refuse to accept the dates the Prophet has asked me to give you?" The man said: "Yes, if justice is not expected of the Prophet, of who else can it be?"

Yes, if a Prophet is not just who else can be? We shall therefore present just one case here.

After the fall of Makkah the Prophet laid siege to Tayif. But it was well fortified and after 3 weeks and a loss of twelve men, he had to lift the siege unconditionally. However, when a man called Sakhar  a wealthy chief of a tribe  learned of the unsuccessful siege he vowed that he would beseige Tayif until the inhabitants surrendered. He surrounded the town with his men and in a few weeks time forced it to surrender. Then he sent his report to the Prophet who was of course much pleased. But then a man followed complaining that his aunt was in Sakhar's possession. The Prophet ordered Sakhar to release her  although she had been captured before the people of Tayif had surrendered. Subsequently members of two clans came up complaining that Sakhar had sieved their water spring in pre Islamic days, but now that they were Muslims, their spring may be returned to them. The Prophet called Sakhar and told him: "Sakhar! When a people accept Islam they become owners of their lives and property. Return to them their spring." Sakhar said: "I shall, O apostle of God." But the narrator says, the Prophet blushed with the thought that on both counts Sakhar had to give in and that he could not reward him for the services he had rendered.[32]

## HUMILITY

Despite the excellent qualities, only some of which we could mention in this short account, he was extremely humble. Once he was asked who it was that was the most honorable. He said it was Yousuf who was the son of a prophet (Ya'qub), a grand son of a prophet (Ishaq) and a great grand son of a prophet (Ibrahim).

[32] After quoting this from Abu Da'ud, Ibn Kathir, however, says that traditionists (*muhaddithun*) disagree over the reliability of the narrators. See *Al Bidaya wa al Nihaya*. vol. 4 p. 352.

Consequently, although he was from a very respectable family, the members of whom kept themselves at a distance from the masses, he used to mix freely with the common people. In Makkah he could be seen sitting for hours chatting with a non Arab hawker at Mount Safa. We also know of the Bedouin who used to send him gifts from the countryside to whom he used to send city wares.

'Ali has reported that once while the Prophet was Praying, he was stung by a scorpion. He said: 'May Allah curse the scorpion. It spares neither one Praying nor anyone else.' This simple incident states volumes on humility. Note the words of the Prophet: 'It spares neither one Praying nor anyone else,' whereas, if he was conscious of the importance of his position he would have said: 'It spares neither "a Prophet" nor anyone else.' During an altercation between a Jew and a Muslim, the Muslim claimed that the Prophet was the best of creatures. The Jew said it was Moses who was the most honored. The Muslim lost his temper and slapped the Jew. The Jew reported to the Prophet. He said: "Do not call me superior to Moses. For, on the Day of Judgement everyone will lose his consciousness. I will be the first to regain mine. And, (as I look about), I will find Moses holding the Pedestal of 'Arsh. Now I do not know if he will regain his consciousness earlier than me, or will not faint at all because of his fainting at the Tur.'[33]

And when somebody addressed him as: "O the best of creations", he said: "The best of creation was Ibrahim."

And this was not only in words. His deeds exceeded his words. Very early in Madinah, when a group of ten *muhajirun* were assigned each to an *ansari* the Prophet himself was one of the ten of a group. A man called Miqdad b. al Aswad was also of the same group. He says, "We had a few goats which we used to milk in the evenings and share the milk. The Prophets's share used to be left in the pot since he came back late in the night. Once I was very hungry and drank away the Prophet's share also. When he came in he found everyone sleeping and the pot empty. He did not complain. He said simply: "O God

---

[33] See the Qur'an, chapter 7, verse 143 for explanation.

feed him  who will feed me today." Miqdad says, "I got up with a knife to slaughter a goat." The Prophet stopped him. The goat was milked again and the Prophet drank whatever it yielded.

Here is another incident which will tell us with greater effect what the Prophet thought of himself and others. He had gone to see Sa'd b. 'Ubadah. When he intended to return Sa'd ordered his son Qays to accompany him on the way back. The Prophet asked Qays to mount his camel. But the lad refused out of deference. The Prophet told him: "Either you will mount my camel or you will return." Qays preferred to return.

Consider now this statement of Anas which should give some idea of the Prophet's greatness: "If the Prophet was invited to a meal of bread made of barley and a soup that had begun to stink, he would respond to the invitation."

## MIRACLES

On several occasions the Prophet was asked to produce a miracle in support of his claim. The demand was more persistent during the Makkan stay, and came both from the Makkan pagans as well as the 'holders of the Book,' the Jews and Christians. The Makkans wanted the mounts Safa and Marwa made of gold, the valleys to be flowing with rivers, the hills surrounding the town and restricting its expansion transferred elsewhere, and the arid lands turned green. Further, if all that could be accomplished, why not bring back to life the dead Qurayshi chiefs who would bear testimony to the truth of the Prophet's claim?! The Jews and Christians wanted miracles similar to those produced by the previous prophets, such as quickening of the dead, healing of the maimed and blind, or transforming of a staff into a snake and so forth.

The invariable reply through revelation was that Muhammad is no more but a human being, like themselves, except that he has been chosen for Apostleship. It is not for Muhammad, therefore, to perform miracles, as it was not for any other prophet of yore. Miracles are always performed by God, whenever He wills and in whatever form He wills. They are not produced in response to challenges thrown at Him or His prophets anyway.[34] They are shown to dispel grave doubts that a people may have. The function of a miracle is to convince the people of the authenticity of the message and the Messenger. In the case of the Prophet this reason did not exist. In his case, the people being addressed were at heart convinced of his prophethood, but denied it due to other reasons. As for those among them who harbored doubts, a miracle had already been revealed: in the form of the Qur'an. It is far greater and more convincing than that of turning a rod into a snake or other kinds of miracles given to previous prophets. The miracles of the previous prophets were useful only for those who personally witnessed those miracles. As for those who were not present, there was nothing for them to check and verify. Whereas the miracle revealed to the Prophet was a perennial one which anyone knowing the language could verify.

What sign could be more manifest than this living miracle? The Prophet was unlettered. He had never received instructions from anyone. For forty years of his life he had lived among the Makkans leading an uneventful life. He was not a poet or an orator. He was not one of those wise bards that appear in every society: whose sayings are repeated in the evening gossips, and whose moral precepts are occasionally followed by the simpler men. He was just an average and ordinary person in everything except that he was a bit generous, and very honest. What happened then after forty long years that he suddenly began to dictate a writing which the literally well developed Arab society could not imitate: neither then nor later? What Power was dictating it to him? Why shouldn't they believe the man whose honesty they had experienced for a long period and whom they used to call "Al Amin" (the trustworthy). Everybody wants to own a thing he has created, whether it be a few lines of poetry or of a piece of art. Why was Muhammad disclaiming the finest piece of writing that scribes have ever scribed?

[34] Note how close Jesus Christ was, who showed several signs to his followers but rarely to the unbelieving, when he said, replying to demands for a sign: "A wicked and adultrous generation seeketh after a sign: and there shall no sign be given unto it..." (Matthew 16: 4)

Moreover, the Revelation itself was throwing a challenge at them to produce a few lines equal in literary excellence, even if not in the power to guide, convince and heal. The fact is that the Quraysh, on whose acceptance or rejection depended the acceptance or rejection of a large number of people, were convinced at heart that it was a Revelation of God. This, as various reports suggest, they acknowledged in private. But if they did not want to acknowledge in public, and accept to follow the Prophet, it was because of some reasons. One was that they were angry that God had not chosen one of their chiefs, an aristocrat, rich and influential man for the office. Muhammad didn't even have a donkey to ride on when he went to Tayif. Another reason was that Islam refused to accept their leadership. In the new system leadership depended on various qualities, and was not hereditary. Again, it had taken the Quraysh many decades to build their hegemony which assured them certain privileges. They did not want to lose it all in one stroke. To be reduced to being equal to all was not a message welcome to them, even if it was from God.

As for the Jews, they too were not going to believe in any prophet who was not from them: an Israelite. They had decided on their own that God was bound by their wishes; that His Guidance must necessarily work through the Jews. It was not important to them what the message itself was: even if it confirmed the teachings of their holy book: the Torah. There was no way for them to accept the Guidance that did not come through an Israeli prophet.

As for the Christians, they had no demands of any special nature. They had found a Messiah in the person of Jesus. With the stroke of a conference in Nicaea Jesus suddenly became what no human being had ever become before: a son of God! Further, according to them, man was so hopelessly wicked that no guidance from God was going to redeem him. Therefore, God finally decided to give birth to a son. Then He sent the son to the earth to be crucified on the cross for the benefit of all the sinners that would follow him   the question of the previous generations kept in abeyance for a moment. Having found the son, they wanted no more, and the mankind needed no more. All that was required was to express the catechism before a priest in the Church that Christ was a son of God. What the new believer did in this world; how he behaved; how he earned his money or spent it, etc., etc., was not a matter of any significance. It was enough to believe that the son of God died on the cross in atonement of man's sins, previous and future, for a man to earn salvation. Therefore, there was no need to go any further on the road looking for guidance.

These were the kind of people that were demanding miracles. What purpose were the miracles going to serve? The answer was obvious. No miracles therefore were performed on their demand, except of course the presentation of the Qur'an itself, which, with its literary merits and teachings, was always there for them to subject to tests.

## THE NOCTURNAL JOURNEY

Yet it was God's mercy to show an additional sign to the unbelievers before they could be condemned and punished. For Allah's message is not such that when it is sent through a prophet, it may or may not be accepted by the people without serious consequences arising from the responses. When it is sent, it must be taken seriously. Therefore, before the condemnation and punishment of those who cried lies, Allah revealed a very convincing sign. It was by way of the Prophet's journey from Makkah to Jerusalem, from there to the Heavens and then back to Makkah, all within one night. This happened a little before the Prophet was ordered to leave Makkah for Madinah. A beast called Burraq, that placed its one foot on earth and the next in the horizon, was brought by Jibril one night and the Prophet was transported on it to Jerusalem. From there he was taken to the Heavens where He was shown the Hell, Paradise, and various other signs of God. He also met various prophets there, and witnessed some people being punished for certain sins, as well as the rewards Allah has prepared in the Paradise for those who believe and do good works. He was also given there the gift of five daily Prayers. Then he was brought back to Jerusalem where he led in Prayers the previous prophets and, finally, he was brought back to Makkah.

The next morning when he spoke of his journey to his aunt, she, although a believer, strongly urged him not to announce this to the Quraysh, for whom, she feared, this might become another point of ridicule. The Prophet pulled his shirt off her clutching hands and left saying, "By God, I shall tell them."

Umm Hani's fears were true. The Quraysh had a good laugh. In fact even some Muslims, weak in faith, turned apostate. The strong in faith were led by Abu Bakr who, when questioned if he still believed in the Prophet, said, "Why not! I believe in greater wonders. I believe that an angel comes down to him revealing the Qur'an." Wary of him and the likes of him, the Quraysh turned to the Prophet. They asked him both serious and absurd questions to which he replied in his usual serious manner. Finally they said: "Alright. You say you have been to Jerusalem. Agreed. Tell us what does Jerusalem look like." Now all the journeys that the Prophet had made to Syria prior to his prophethood were in the company of Quraysh. And they knew that he had never been into Jerusalem. So they thought that at least once they had caught him on the wrong foot. But to their surprise he described the city in such detail as if it was before his eyes. In fact it was then before him, as explained the Prophet himself later. For when they asked certain details, which only a person who had visited the city several times could have answered, Allah brought the city before the Prophet's eyes, so that he looked into it and answered their questions.

He also told them that while on his way back from Jerusalem a camel of a caravan, passing through such and such a valley, had bolted away "and I showed them where it hid." Also, on the way back to Makkah, he had passed by a caravan that had kept some water in a pitcher during the night halt. He had drunk the water and replaced its lid. The caravan itself was now advancing towards Makkah and was headed by a camel loaded with such and such goods. To the amazement of the Quraysh the caravan did arrive headed by the same kind of camel as described by the Prophet, and the people in it admitted that the pitcher was found empty despite the lid. Later, when the other caravan was also back they enquired about the camel that had bolted away, and they said, "Quite right. A camel had bolted away and we had heard a man calling us to it so that we were able to recover it!"

We have stated above that miracles are revealed by God to help a people in grave doubts about the authenticity of the message or the Messenger. They have another function. Sometimes they take place to help the faithful in a difficult situation or to increase their faith. These other kind of miracles that took place at the hands of the Prophet by the will of Allah, occurred mainly during the Madinan period. Here we present a few.

## INCREASE IN FOOD

When the Muslims got news of the advancing Arab armies towards Madinah, in the third year after *hijrah*, they were passing through a very difficult economic phase. When they began to dig the trench, some of them had stones tied to their stomachs to ward off hunger and keep their backs straight. When they complained to the Prophet, he showed them his own stomach which had two stones tied to it. One evening, when everyone was preparing to go home after the day's digging, a Companion, 'Abdullah b. Rawaha, invited the Prophet to dinner. He had meant to invite only the Prophet because all that he had was a little meat and some bread. But when the Prophet received the invitation, he ordered a crier to announce that dinner for everyone was going to be in the house of 'Abdullah b. Rawaha. 'Abdullah b. Rawaha was of course much embarrassed, but did not have the courage to protest. All he could say was, "To Allah we all belong, and to Him we shall return." Everyone of course followed him to his house. Once in, 'Abdullah placed the meager food before the Prophet, who invoked Allah's name and began to eat. A group of people was with him. When they were finished, they left and another group took their place. Group after group entered, ate and left, until everyone had eaten. 'Abdullah b. Rawaha says that when they were all finished, he and his wife didn't know if the left over was more in quantity or that which they had originally placed before the Prophet!

# INCREASE IN WATER

During the return journey from Tabuk, the Prophet and his people ran short of water. The Prophet knew of a watering place and instructed the people not to draw water from the spring until he had arrived. But some people who reached the place earlier drew water from it so that by the time the Prophet arrived it had shrunk to nothing but a small muddy pool. He was angry that water had been drawn before his arrival. However, whatever little was there in it was collected and brought to the Prophet. He washed his hands and face in the bowl and threw the water back into the spring. Suddenly water began to gush forth from the spring and everybody drew from it sufficient for his needs. They were then many thousands in number.

A similar incident occurred not far from Madinah on a different occasion. It was the afternoon Prayer time and people were unable to find water. When they had lost all hopes of finding water they reported to the Prophet. He asked them to bring a (large) bowl of water. When it was brought he thrust his hands up to the wrist into it and water began to spring out of his fingers. Everyone of the Companions was able to make ablution with it and drink to his fill. They were then about eighty souls.

# Chapter 5

# SOME OF HIS SAYINGS

## Intentions

1. Deeds are by intentions. Everyone shall have that which he intended for. [35]

## The Natural State

2. Every human being is born on nature (that is, incorrupt, and believing in One God). It is his parents who Judaize him, Christianize him or Zoroastrianize him.[36]

## The Simple Demand

3. Allah will address the least suffering man of Hell and ask: 'Would you, if you had all the treasures of the world, ransom it to escape this punishment?' The man will say: 'Yes indeed.' Allah will say, 'My demand on you was of a less exacting nature. I had instructed you all when you were yet in Adam's back not to ascribe partners unto Me. But you refused and ascribed partners unto Me.'[37]

---

[35] That is, a man gets rewarded for his actions according to his intentions. If he intends rewards of the Hereafter, then that is for him. If he intends immediate worldly rewards, he is given that, sooner or later in measure commensurate to his efforts. So also, if he intends to please God, God is pleased with him. But if he intends to please others, his actions are turned to them who reward him in the manner they think fit. The hadith is from Bukhari.

[36] Bukhari.

[37] The reference here is to the pledge taken by Allah from Adam's progeny in their pre natal stage to the effect that they shall not ascribe partners unto Allah  See the Qur'an chapter 7, verses 172 4. Bukhari and Muslim.

## The Essence of Faith

4.  He who loved for God, hated for God, gave for God and denied for God, perfected his faith.[38]

## Hypocrisy

5.  These three are the signs of a hypocrite even if he Prays and fasts: 'When he speaks, he lies, when he promises, he breaks it, and, when he is trusted, he deceives.'[39]

## Islam

6.  (The house of) Islam rests on five (pillars): the testimony that God is One and Muhammad is his bondman and Prophet, establishment of Prayers, payment of zakah, (performance) of hajj, and, (observation of) Ramadan fasts'.[40]

## Practice

7.  People! There is nothing that will take you nearer to Paradise and away from the Fire, but I have bid you do it. And there is nothing that will take you nearer to the Fire and away from Paradise but I have forbidden it. And *Ruh 'l Amin* (according to another report, *Ruh 'l Quds*)[41] put it in my heart that no soul shall die until it has obtained its share of the world. Fear then Allah and adopt fair means in seeking (your share of) the world. And let not any delay in its coming compel you to seek it through disobedience of God. For what is with Him cannot be had but through His obedience.[42]

## Good Conduct

8.  The best in faith of the faithful are those that are best in conduct. Indeed good conduct can attain the status of Prayer and fasts.[43]

---

[38]  Abu Da'ud, Tirmizi.

[39]  *Al Jami' Al Saghir*, Suyuti, no. 3473. Some words have been dropped following Manawi's notes.

[40]  Bukhari and Muslim.

[41]  Jibril has been meant by both the terms.

[42]  *Sharh 'l Sunnah*, Bayhaqi, *Kalam*. p 229.

[43]  *Al Ahadith Al Sahiha*, Albani, no. 1590.

## Asceticism

9.  Asceticism is not to treat the lawful as unlawful or to waste away one's wealth. Rather, asceticism is to treat that which is with Allah as more trustworthy than that which is in your possession; and that the rewards that you earn when a misfortune befalls you be dearer to you, were that misfortune to continue.[44]

## Waste of Time

10. It is the sign of a man's good faith that he does not indulge in that which is not of his concern.[45]

## Prudence

11. A believer cannot be stung from the same hole twice.[46]

## Strength

12. A strong believer is better and dearer to Allah than a weak one. Although, in each there is (some) good. Be on the look out for what will be of profit to you. Don't weaken down (in its search). However, if things don't go your way, say, 'Allah's predetermination. He did what He willed.' And beware of 'If.' For, 'if' opens the door for the Devil.[47]

## Deterioration

13. 'These hearts also get rusted as does iron when it comes in contact with water'. It was asked: 'And how are they to be cleansed O apostle of God?' He said: 'Through much remembrance of death and recitation of the Qur'an.[48]

14. Allah will not withdraw knowledge gradually, withdrawing it from the people in a recondite manner. Rather, He will withdraw knowledge by withdrawing the scholars. So that when scholars are not left, people will consult the ignorant

---

[44]  Ibn Majah, no. 4100.
[45]  Ibid, no.3976.
[46]  Ibid, no.3982.
[47]  Ibid, no. 4168.
[48]  Bayhaqi in *Sho'b al Iman, Kalam*, p.340.

leaders. They will give their opinion without knowledge. Thus they will misguide them and themselves.[49]

## The Effects of Good Deeds

15. (A Muslim's) age does not increase but by good deeds, and nothing will repel the predetermined save supplications. And verily, a man is denied provision (written in his name) but because of an evil deed that he does.[50]

## The Clear Way

16. I have left you on a clear, shiny path whose night is (as bright) as its day. No one will swerve away from it but will destroy himself. He who lives after me will witness lots of differences. Upon you (in such circumstances) is to hold fast unto my ways that you know and the ways of the rightly guided Caliphs after me. Hold on to that by your teeth. And upon you is obedience: even if it (the governing person) were to be an Abyssinian slave. For a believer is like a tamed camel. He moves in the direction he is led to.[51]

## The Individual and the Society

17. The believer who mixes with people and bears their wrongs with patience is better than he who does not mix with them and does not bear their wrongs with patience.[52]

## Usury

18. Usury has seventy grades. The least of them (in foulness) is like a man having intercourse with his mother.[53]

## Oppression

19. Beware of the oppressed man's cry. It rises to God as fast as a sparkle (from fire).[54]

---

[49] Ibn Majah, no.52.
[50] Ibid, no. 90.
[51] Ibid, no. 43.
[52] *Al Ahadith Al Sahiha*, Albani, no.939.
[53] Ibid, no. 1871.
[54] *Jami' Saghir*, no.149.

## Health and Wealth

20. Wealth is not harmful for him who fears God, while good health for one who fears God is better than wealth. And, to be of a cheerful disposition is a bounty (of God).[55]

## Gratefulness

21. He who does not thank the people will not thank God.[56]

## Socializing

22. The best of food in the eyes of God is that on which many hands fall.[57]

## The Despicable Man

23. Verily Allah despises every proud, avaricious man (who is) quarrelsome in the markets, a log in the night, a donkey in the day, clever in worldly matters but ignorant of the hereafter.[58]

## The Believer

24. The faithful is like a date palm tree. He remains green all the year round.[59]

## Shame

25. If you have no shame then do as you please.[60]

## The Ultimate Loyalty

26. There is (to be) no obedience of the created in the disobedience of the Creator.[61]

[55] Albani, no.174.

[56] Abu Da'ud, Tirmizi.

[57] *Jami' Saghir* no.213. And the meaning of the hadith is that God likes people sharing their food with as many as they can, thus co mingling with them.

[58] Albani no.195.

[59] Adopted from Bukhari, *Kitab 'l `Ilm*.

[60] Bukhari, *Kitab 'al Anbiya'*.

[61] *Sharh Al Sunnah*, Kalam p 228.

## Gossip

27. It is enough of a lie for a man to repeat all that he hears. And it is enough for a man to be a miser to say: 'I will take all my right and shall forego none of it.'[62]

## Animals

28. Mount these beasts unharmingly and dismount them unharmingly. Do not make chairs out of them.[63]

29. When you return to your people tell them to feed these animals well. Tell them also to shorten their nails in order not to hurt them in their udders when milking.[64]

## Plants

30. If the Day of judgement is called out while one of you is holding a sapling in his hand, then if he can plant it before presenting himself (for judgement), let him do it.[65]

## Natural Resources

31. Do not use excess water even at a running stream.[66]

## Distances

32. Verily between the two leaves (of the door of) the Paradise is the travel distance of forty years.[67]

---

[62] *Jami' Saghir*: no.6244.

[63] The Prophet said those words when he saw some people mounted on their beasts and engaged in conversation. Albani, no.21.

[64] A man called Sumadah b. Rabi' asked the Prophet for some financial help. He gave him a few camels and advised him in these words. Albani, no.317.

[65] Albani, no.931.

[66] Ibn Majah, h.425 (*Al Taharah*).

[67] Meaning: it is so wide. Note the time scale. Albani, no.1698.

[67] Ibid, no.109. It is not known what exactly is meant by *Kursi* and *'Arsh*. The hadith merely explains how large the unknown is compared to the known.

# Sizes

33. The seven heavens (meaning the created world) compared to the *Kursi* are not but like a ring thrown in a large field. And the *'Arsh* in comparison to the *Kursi* is as large as the field compared to the ring.[68]

## Mercy

34. When God had brought His creations into being, He wrote down in His Book about Himself, and the Book remains with Him in the Heavens, 'Verily My mercy exceeds My anger.'[69]

# The Times

35. Allah the Mighty, the Exalted says: 'Son of Adam abuses Me. He curses the times. Indeed I am the Time: in My Hand is the Command and I shuffle the days and nights.'[70]

# Tests

36. A man is tested according to the strength of his faith. If he is strong in it, the test can be severe. But if he is weak it can be mild: so that afflictions do not depart from a man but leave him walking on earth without a sin on him.[71]

# Jihad

37. He who died without ever having fought (in the way of Allah), nor having ever made firm intentions about it, died on a branch of hypocrisy.[72]

---

[68] Ibid, no.109. It is not known what exactly is meant by *Kursi* and *'Arsh*. The hadith merely explains how large the unknown is compared to the known.

[69] Bukhari, *Kitab al Tawhid*.

[70] Bukhari, *Tafsir surah Al Jathiyyah*.

[71] *Jami' Saghir*, no.1054.

[72] Muslim, *Kitab Al Imarah*. Literally, jihad is to exert the most and put in one's best efforts into a cause. Islamically, jihad has many levels. The first is to struggle with one's own self to overcome the base desires and replace them with the love of God and His Messenger. The second is to exert one's utmost pressure on the society to change it for the better. Yet another is to fight in the Cause of Allah, if that is the demand of the situation.

## Prevention of the Evil

38. The first deterioration that set in among the Israelites is
    that one of them would commit an evil. His friend would
    discourage him by saying: 'O so and so. Don't do that, for you
    know that that is not allowed.' But when he saw him
    committing it again, he wouldn't stop him, because they
    would be friends, eating and drinking together and
    interacting in various ways. When they did that, then Allah
    transformed the heart of some as like that of the others (ie.
    all became corrupt).[73]

## The House of Praise

39. When a man's child dies Allah says to the angels: 'You have
    seized my slave's child?!' They reply: 'Yes'. He says: 'You have
    seized the darling of his heart?!' They reply: 'Yes'. He says:
    'And what did My slave have to say?' They reply: 'He praised
    you and said: 'Verily we belong to God and to Him do we return.'
    Allah Most High says then: 'Build a house for My slave in
    Paradise and call it the "House of Praise."'[74]

## Fabricators

40. He who attributed to me what I did not say may make his
    dwelling in the Fire.[75]

---


[73] Abu Da'ud, no.4336.
[74] Ibid, no.854.
[75] Bukhari, *Kitab al 'Ilm.*

# Chapter 6

# PRAYER WORDS, AND PROPHECIES

## SOME OF HIS PRAYER WORDS

1.  O God: Grant me all things that are good: that I know of and that which I do not know of; and save me from all evil: that I know if and that which I do not know of.[76]

2.  Lord! Grant me: all the effects that spring forth from Your Mercy and from Your Forgiveness; rescue from all sins; a part from all that is virtuous; entry into Paradise and deliverance from the Fire.[77]

3.  Lord! I seek Your protection from: weakness, indolence, cowardice, parsimony, old age, punishment in the grave, and trials at the hands of Dajjal. Lord! Grant me Thou my soul (*nafs*) its piety and purify it, verily Thou art the best of those that purify it. Thou art its true Friend and true Master.

    Lord! I seek Your refuge from knowledge that does not benefit, from a heart that does not submit, from an appetite that is not satiated, and from a prayer that is not answered.[78]

## SOME OF HIS PROPHECIES

1.  Islam started as a stranger and will become a stranger again. So blessed be the estranged. It was asked: 'Who are the estranged?' He said: '(Those who become so) due to <u>disagreements</u> between the people'.[79]

[76] *Jami' Saghir*, Suyuti, no 1455.

[77] Ibid, no.1474.

[78] Ibid, no.155.

[79] Those seem to have been meant whose relations get strained with the people due to them taking Islam seriously   Allah knows best. The hadith is from Muslim as quoted by Ibn Kathir in his 'Alamat Yaum al Qiyamah.

2. With the Hour approaching, there will be no increase in the people but in their greed, and there will be no increase in the people but their drift away from God.[80]

3. Soon Euphrates will reveal mountains of gold. News will spread and people will advance towards it. The locals will say, 'If we take no action these people will take away everything.' So they will fight over it and only one in hundred will survive the war.[81]

4. By Him in whose hands is my soul the world will not come to pass till a day comes when the murderer will not know why he killed and the murdered why he was killed.[82]

5. The Prophet was asked by a bedouin about when the last Hour would arrive. He said, 'When trust is lost, expect the Last Hour'. The man asked, 'And how will trust be lost?' He said: 'When affairs of the people are entrusted to those that are unworthy of it, then expect the Last Hour.'[83]

6. The Last Hour will not arrive before wealth becomes abundant and overflowing; before a man brings the zakah due on his property and cannot find anyone to accept it; and before the land of the Arabs returns to the state of meadows and rivers.[84]

7. There has been no prophet who did not warn his people about the One eyed Liar (Dajjal or Antichrist). I tell you that he will be one eyed. And your Lord is not one eyed. On his forehead will be written 'Kafir'.[85]

---

[80] Albani, no.1510.

[81] Muslim, Kitab al Fitan.

[82] *Mishkat*, on the authority of Muslim.

[83] Bukhari, *Kitab al Fitan*.

[84] Mishkat al Masabih on the authority of Muslim.

[85] "Your Lord is not one eyed"; because Antichrist will claim to be God. Bukhari, *Fitan*.

8.  Prophets are brothers of the same father   their religion is one   only mothers are different.[86] I am nearest to Jesus (on whom be peace) since between us there was no prophet. And (be sure that) he is going to come (again). You should recognize him when you see him: he will be of medium height, of complexion fair and red, wearing two pinkish cloaks, hair straight and so shiny that even when not wet you would think water was dripping off them   he will break the cross, destroy the pig, annul *jizyah* (poll tax levied on non Muslims),[87] invite people to Islam so that during his tenure God will destroy all religions except Islam, and in his time God will destroy Dajjal also. This will be followed by a spell of peace on earth during which lions and camels, leopards and cows, wolves and sheep will graze and move together. Children will play with snakes and be not hurt. Such will be the state for the next forty years. Then Jesus will die and Muslims will pray over him (and bury him).[88]

9.  This *ummah* (the community of Muslims) will always remain true to Islam. Those that confront them will do them no (real) harm   until the Day of Judgement is pronounced.[89]

[86]  That is, the *Shari'ah.* are different although the religions are same.

[87]  That is, at his hands people will either accept Islam or be destroyed at his hand.

[88]  Ibn Kathir in his *'Alamat Yaum al Qiyamah* on the authority of Ahmad.

[89]  Bukhari, *Fitan.* Other reports specify the *"ummah"* as one section of the *ummah* that will remain fighting the other communities over Islam.

# BIBLIOGRAPHY

*'Ahad e Nabawi Ke Maidan e Jung,* (Urdu), Dr. Hamidullah, Deoband India, 102p.

*'Alāmāt e Qiyamat Wa Nuzul e Masih,* (Urdu), Muhammad Rafi' 'Usmani, Maktabah Darul 'Ulum, Karachi, 1401 A.H., 176 p

*'Alamat Yowm Al Qiyamah,* (Arabic), Hafiz Ibn Kathir, ed. Abd Al Latif, Cairo, 1980, 142p.

*Al Arba'in, Al Nawawi,* (Arabic), Yahya Ibn Sherfuddin Nawawi, Dar Al Qur'an Al Karim, Saudi Arabia. 1979, 127p.

*Al Durr Al Manthur Fi Tafsir bi Al Mathur,* (Arabic), Jalaluddin Al Suyuti.

*Al Bidaya Wa Al Nihaya,* (Arabic), Hafiz Ibn Kathir, 14 vols., Maktabah Al Ma'arif, Beirut,

*Faid Al Qadir, Sharh Al Jami' Al Saghir,* (Arabic), Jalaluddin Al Suyuti, ed. 'Abdul Ra'uf Al Munawi, 6 vols., Dar Al Baz, Makkah Al Mukarramah.

*Fiqh Al Sirah,* (Arabic), Munir Muhammad Ghadban, Jami'ah Umm al Qura, Makkah al Mukarramah.

*Kalām e Nubuwwat,* (Urdu), Vol.I, Muhammad Farooq Khan, Maktabah Markazi Islami, Delhi.

*Muhammad,* (English), Martin Lings, Suhail Academy, Lahore, 1983, 359p.

*Rahmat e 'Alam,* (Urdu), S.Abul Hasan Ali Nadwi, Maktabah Nashr Wa 'Isaha'at e Islam, Lucknow.

*Safwat At Tafāsir,* (Arabic), 3 vols, Muhammad 'Ali Al Sabuni, Dar Al Qur'an Karim, Beirut.

*Sahih Bukhari,* (Urdu), 6 vols., Deeni Kutub Khanah, Lahore, Pakistan.

*Sahih Muslim,* (Arabic), ed. Imam Nawawi, 12 vols., Al Mataba'ah Misriyyah Wa Matabatuha.

*Silsilah Al Ahādith Al Sahihah,* (Arabic), 4 vols., Muhammad Nasiruddin Albani, Al Maktabah Al Islami, Kuwait.

*Siratun Nabiyy,* (Urdu), 6 vols., Shibli Nu'mani and Syed Sulaiman Nadwi, Dar Al Musannifin Azamgarh, India.

*Sunan Abi Da'ud,* ('Aun al Ma'bud), 14 vols., Dar al Fikr, Lebanon.

*Sunan Ibn Majah,* (Arabic), ed. Fu'ad 'Abdul Baqi, 2 vols., Maktabah 'Ilmiyyah, Lebanon.

*Sunan Al Tirmidhi,* (Arabic), 10 vols., ed. Mubarakpuri, (Tuhfat Al Ahwazi), Dar Al Fikr.

*Tafsir Al Qur'an Al 'Azim,* (Arabic), 4 vols. Ibn Kathir, Dar Al Fikr, Cairo.

*The Life of Muhammad,* (English), Ibn Ishaq (*Sirah Rasulullah*), Tr. Alfred Guilluame, Oxford Univ. Press, Karachi, 1978, 813p.

*The Life of Muhammad,* (English), Muhammad Husayn Haykal, Tr. Isma'il Raja'i A. al Faruqi, North American Trust Publications, 1970, 640p.

*Zād Al Ma'ād,* (Arabic), Ibn Qayyim, 4 vols. Mu'assa sah Al Risalah, Cairo, 1985.

*Zawjāt Al Nabiyy Al Tahirāt,* (Arabic), Muhammad Mahmud Sawwaf, Darul I'tisam, Cairo, p.96.

# INDEX

# S

Sa'd, b. 'Ubadah 51, 85
Safa, mount 81, 84 1
Safyah 59
Sakhar 83
Sauda 57 8
Shirwayh 79
Sumaiyyah 80
Suwaybit 78
Syria 3, 6, 28 9, 41 3, 72, 91

# T

Tabuk 32, 53, 90
Tayif 2, 13, 28, 50 1, 79, 83
Torah 25, 37, 87
Trinity 24, 26, 49
Trinity Valley 2

# U

Uhud 34 5, 59, 70 1, 77 81
'Umar, ibn al Khattab 35 6, 40, 56, 58, 73, 81
Umm al Fadl 32
Umm Habibah 59, 75 4
Umm Hakim 32
Umm Hani 89
Umm Ma'bad 66
Umm Salamah 61
'Umrah 40, 63
'Uthman, ibn 'Affan 12

# W

Waraqah, ibn Naufal 8
Wahriz 77
Wahshi 81

# Y

Ya'qub, the Prophet 84
Yethrib 2, 12, 17 9, 23
Yemen 1 3, 42, 69, 75, 77 5
Yousuf, the Prophet 10, 84

# Z

Zayd, b. Thabit 10, 62
Zaynab, bint Jahash 61, 2
Zaynab, bin Khuzaymah 61
Zuhri, ibn Shihab 42